Librarian's Guide to Writing for Professional Publication

Librarian's Guide to Writing for Professional Publication

Marta Mestrovic Deyrup

LIBRARIES UNLIMITED™

An Imprint of ABC-CLIO, LLC

Santa Barbara, California • Denver, Colorado

Library of Congress Cataloging-in-Publication Data

Names: Deyrup, Marta Mestrovic, author.
Title: Librarian's guide to writing for professional publication / Marta
   Mestrovic Deyrup.
Description: Santa Barbara, California : Libraries Unlimited, 2019. |
   Includes bibliographical references and index.
Identifiers: LCCN 2018035660 (print) | LCCN 2018051933 (ebook) | ISBN
   9781440837692 (ebook) | ISBN 9781440837685 (pbk. : acid-free paper)
Subjects: LCSH: Library science—Authorship. | Library science
   literature—Publishing. | Authorship—Problems, exercises, etc.
Classification: LCC Z669.7 (ebook) | LCC Z669.7 .D49 2019 (print) | DDC
   808.06/602—dc23
LC record available at https://lccn.loc.gov/2018035660

ISBN: 978-1-4408-3768-5 (paperback)
       978-1-4408-3769-2 (ebook)

23 22 21 20 19   1 2 3 4 5

This book is also available as an eBook.

Libraries Unlimited
An Imprint of ABC-CLIO, LLC

ABC-CLIO, LLC
130 Cremona Drive, P.O. Box 1911
Santa Barbara, California 93116-1911
www.abc-clio.com

This book is printed on acid-free paper ∞

Manufactured in the United States of America

To Curtis Alden Deyrup, who taught me how to write

Contents

Preface

Years ago, when my children were very small, I worked as a freelance writer for *Publishers Weekly*, mainly doing book reviews and author interviews. Eventually, my editor gave me my first big assignment, covering a conference on dissident Czech authors at NYU. This was in 1990, just shortly after the Velvet Revolution. I attended literary panels, conducted interviews, and in short had an absolutely thrilling time. But when I got home and sat down to write the article, I began to panic. I had no idea how to structure a newspaper article, in fact I didn't even know what the lead was. After several hours of half-hearted attempts at writing, I simply handed all my notes to my husband, who at that time was the managing editor of a trade newspaper. He sat down with me, and we (really, he) wrote the article. After we had finished, he said, "Now that I've shown you what to do, you don't need me. You'll be able to do this yourself from now on." And I did, although in the beginning it was slow going at best.

This book is called *Librarian's Guide to Writing for Professional Publication* because the kind of writing we do as librarians is not an art, it's a craft. And any kind of craft takes some practice to get right. I hope this book can provide you with some of the support I received when I began to write and that you will be successful in all your writing endeavors.

Acknowledgment

Thanks to my editor, Blanche Woolls, for the help she provided with this book and also to Barbara Ittner for suggesting this topic.

ONE

Introduction

It may seem as though writing doesn't have much to do with professional librarianship. But if you think about it, this really isn't the case. It is hard to imagine running a successful library of any type without documenting the activities that take place inside it. Even if you are not an academic librarian or a library and information science (LIS) professor who needs publications for promotion and tenure, you will, in the course of your career, write hundreds of memos, reports, and e-mails. You may be asked to write a technical manual for your staff, contribute to the library's annual report, or create a newsletter for your library. If you haven't done much writing, this can seem daunting.

This book starts with the premise that to be a successful writer, you don't need to enroll in a writing course or attend a workshop. While any kind of activity that makes you use your writing "muscles" is good—and that includes reading the professional literature to keep up in your field—it isn't necessary in order to successfully communicate with your coworkers, staff, patrons, and vendors. Once you realize that there are only a few kinds of documents used in the workplace and that you can, with a little effort, learn what makes each distinctive, you will be able to apply the principles outlined in this book to your own work. Is it a formulaic approach to writing? Of course. Does it work? Absolutely!

You will need to master about a dozen or so basic document types discussed in this book. In each case, I've tried to include a generic template and/or a more detailed example that you can customize and make you own. Successful professional writing, however, involves more than slavishly following a template. Once you've established the structure of your writing, you can focus on what really matters—the content of your work.

Oddly enough, beginning with a framework is actually a help rather than a hindrance to writing. The simplest explanation for this has to do with cognitive psychology—human beings instinctively look for patterns in order to process and make sense of information, and a template is, by its definition, a master pattern.

CHANNELS OF COMMUNICATION

Writing professionally—that is, communicating in a meaningful way to your colleagues about the work you do—is not a class taught in the LIS school program. Most likely it was assumed that you would learn how to write on the job or that you had picked up enough instruction in your college English courses to get by. Instead of teaching you how to write, your LIS professors probably focused on topics such as knowledge organization, information structures, or reference sources—the services that form the bread and butter of our professional work. Those courses served you well, because if you are reading this book, most likely you are working in some kind of knowledge organization as a librarian, archivist, information broker, or technologist, or you are preparing for a career as one.

Your attitude toward writing, if you've thought about it at all, is probably a result of the kind of education you received. If you are over 40, you probably took classes in middle school and high school that focused on grammar and syntax. This may have included diagramming sentences and memorizing spelling and punctuation rules. If you are under 40, you probably did not formally study grammar at all. Instead you focused on developing communication skills. You might not have done much writing, using other media to express your ideas, such as video, which requires a very different "visual" grammar. You also probably did not learn spelling rules or any other kind of rule for that matter, since at some point in your career you switched entirely to working on a computer, and functions like spelling and grammar were taken over by programs like spell-check. If you are under 35, you probably communicate primarily by texting. Texting has profoundly changed the way we use the written word. The "grammar" of texting includes emojis, abbreviations, and sentence fragments. Texting is really a form of shorthand. If you are in a LIS program right now, you may be learning about multimedia writing. Multimedia writing combines traditional methods of writing, such as a textual narrative, with multimedia (graphics) and dynamic hyperlinks.

The reason that conventional methods of communication are changing has to do with the impact of the Web on almost every aspect of modern life. Thirty or so years ago, the Web was still in its infancy. Unicode had not yet been created, which meant that non-Western European scripts like Chinese and Russian could not be displayed. Coding was done by hand in HTML, and the clarity of an image depended on the resolution and screen size of the computer monitor. Web 1.0 was a "read only" environment, which means there wasn't much you could do with HTML pages, except save and print them. Then things began to accelerate. By 2004, Web pages no longer were static documents. Instead they were part of a growing, interactive environment known as Web 2.0. Web 2.0 allowed people to communicate, post, and shop on the Internet. For the past few years, we have been in a transitional period known as Web 3.0 or the Semantic Web, during which the protocols for communication and the transfer of information are being standardized still further.

The rapid development of the Web as a platform for the delivery of content already has changed how we do writing as a profession. Because the Web is so visually oriented, text can take on characteristics and functions that used to be the purview of graphics. This harkens back to the manuscript tradition of medieval Europe in which images and texts referenced each other as part of a larger narrative. One of the more extreme examples of this is the 2014 University of Virginia annual report.[1] Annual reports generally consist of text accompanied by illustrations, such as charts and tables. The 41-page 2014 University of Virginia annual report, on the other hand, is organized as a visual presentation, completely bypassing the traditional text-driven format. While it is still not clear whether this kind of graphic rendition of textual material is a trend or long-term development, it bears considering whether this is one sign as to whether the written word and graphics are indeed morphing into a new genre of communication.

What is certain is that many of the conventions we are accustomed to will not exist in 20 or 30 years' time. It is quite possible that, in the future, the written word—the oldest form of nonverbal communication—will no longer be the most important method for sending and receiving information. Instead it may be replaced by new hybrid channels of communication. That being said, at this point in time, no matter which generation you come from or what kind of medium you feel the most comfortable using, you still need to be able to communicate through conventional means. That means the written word. It is still the principal method by which all professions exchange ideas and information.

Being able to write well should be part of your tool kit, just like mastering the latest technology or marketing your library through social media. Although you may feel that your talents lie elsewhere, remember that writing is an activity you've done all your life. If you are in graduate school, you've completed countless written assignments. If you now are working in the profession, you are accustomed to writing letters, memos, and reports—the core document types discussed in this book.

Writing well is perhaps the most important skill you can develop in our profession. It can help you shape the direction of what goes on at work, and if done strategically, you can use your writing skills to affect all sorts of positive changes in your professional life. Writing gives the spoken word authority and weight. You meet with your staff to discuss how they will handle a particular incident and then memorialize your instructions in the form of a memo. You do this because it is much more likely the staff will comply than if you just give them a verbal directive. You need to clear up a misunderstanding with a colleague, and you e-mail him an invite to a working lunch. Attached is a brief agenda of what you'd like to discuss. Both of you now have to prepare for this meeting.

Anyone who writes as part of his or her job or classroom responsibilities can benefit from reading this book; however, its intended audience is the information specialist. It is written from the perspective of someone who has 20 years of professional experience in academic libraries. But I've also had a career as writing teacher and book and magazine editor, so I understand the process from all three perspectives.

I know how difficult it is to write, and I'd like to share with you something that I haven't told many people. The students I taught and the writers I edited over the years have often been so anxious about making a mistake or being caught out as a "bad" writer that they've spent needless hours worrying, many times to the detriment of the project they were trying to finish. Some became so preoccupied by what they perceived as the inadequacy of their own writing that they were unable to get beyond the first or second paragraph. All of them were highly educated people, who had no trouble expressing themselves verbally. Even if they were experts on a topic, they often struggled to find the right words to convey what they wanted to say. If you recognize yourself in this description, don't worry. I will try to give you as many strategies as I can to help you overcome these doubts and insecurities.

I consider these obstacles not to be the fault of the writer but of an educational system that places more emphasis on assessment than on teaching writing as a practical skill. There are historical reasons for this. Our current ideas about education were developed in the 20th century when the majority of our country's population became literate. We embraced new theories of learning and ignored the fact that, for most of history, societies depended on the oral transmission of knowledge. If an individual needed to remember information, he or she used a mnemonic technique now referred to as the memory palace. The memory palace consisted of a series of mental prompts that allowed an individual to store and retrieve large amounts of information. There are many pieces of magnificent literature that were passed down to us in this fashion, such as Homer's *Iliad* and the Sanskrit *Vedas.*

In the late 19th and early 20th century, written communication gradually became the dominant medium through which knowledge was shared and preserved. Oral communication was devalued, as was the ability to memorize and store information. This is unfortunate, because auditory learning is always present in our consciousness and can be tapped into at any time. A central thesis of this book is that you can use multiple methods to help you write better and more professionally. If you are having trouble putting words down on paper, tapping into your auditory memory may be a good strategy. It is an often-overlooked technique, probably because hearing is one of those senses—like smell—that we no longer rely on much. Sight, the dominant sense of perception used for reading, is much more important in modern life.

TAP INTO YOUR AUDITORY MEMORY

An example of an auditory learner is my former student Peter. He was unable to write a paragraph, let alone a sentence that was intelligible to the reader. Misdiagnosed as having a learning disability, Peter was placed in special education classes in elementary school. It was not until junior high, after more testing, that he was identified as a having a near genius IQ. By the time he got to college, he had the reputation of being a very bright but unfocused student who was always late with his assignments—a C student at best. But because he was obviously so intelligent and so charming, he managed to get himself into the honors program at our university. I was assigned to be the faculty advisor for his senior thesis—a graduation requirement for the program.

Peter realized he had a problem with time management, and we decided that he needed to use the whole year to work on his thesis, as opposed to the usual semester. He began his research by reading voraciously until he had branched out into all sorts of areas related to his topic—philosophy, linguistics, and history. Although he was unable to formulate his thoughts on paper, he could explain them perfectly in conversation. Peter was one of those rare individuals who could speak in whole sentences and paragraphs. His writing on the other hand was rambling, disorganized, and lacked any of the brilliant observations of his conversations.

Peter and I hit upon the idea of having him think out loud and put his words down on paper as he spoke them. He would literally dictate his thesis to himself. It worked brilliantly. He managed to complete his thesis on time and learned that he could turn one of his strengths, oral communication, into an asset.

If you feel this is an isolated example, put this to the test. Think of a story that has recently been given prominence in the news. Give yourself three minutes to write a summary of what you remember. Take a look at what you've put down. Does your writing make sense? Did you have trouble thinking of the right words to use? Could you have used more time to rewrite and polish what you had to say?

Now take the same news story and do the same thing, only this time verbalize your thoughts as you are writing. If this is hard to do, imagine that a friend or family member is sitting across from you, and you are talking directly to him or her. When you are finished, compare your first and second attempt. Which was easier to do? Which version better reflected what you meant to say? Which was more grammatically correct? Which was better stylistically? Odds are that you felt better about the second attempt because you wrote down what sounded natural to you.

The reason auditory memory works has to do with the way we acquire language as children. You learned to speak by imitating your parents and siblings. In the beginning you made errors of grammar and pronunciation. It was only through constant repetition and correction that you learned how to communicate in a way that others could understand. By the time you were four or five, you had grasped the syntax of a simple English sentence (i.e., subject–verb–object) and the patterns of regular verbs (e.g., work, worked, have worked) and irregular verbs (e.g., ring, rang, rung).

As I did research, I came to realize the inordinate role writing plays in American education. Unlike reading, which is a solitary pursuit and often deeply pleasurable, writing from the early grades on is done not as form of creative expression but in order to complete an assignment that is almost always graded. How good a writer you are determines how you advance through our educational system. Unless you are a star athlete and receive a sports scholarship or score fabulously well on your SAT or ACT test, your essay for the college application is probably the most important factor in determining whether and where you go to college. If you are in graduate school, your grades will come principally from written assignments. This continues throughout your professional career as you apply for a job or teaching position, fill out grant applications, write reports, or do research when you are an academic. Because of this, people have developed a fear of being judged through their writing that lasts throughout their entire lives. It can be deeply crippling.

Frustration and a sense of inadequacy are probably the two emotions that cause beginning writers the most problems. The good news is it doesn't have to be that way. Let's take a look at five rules I believe are essential to becoming a confident and successful writer.

THE FIVE RULES OF PROFESSIONAL WRITING

RULE #1 THE GOOD ENOUGH PRINCIPLE

The first rule of professional writing is that your work only needs to be good enough. Good enough doesn't mean that you don't set high standards for yourself or try your hardest. It means that you acknowledge that you can only work up to the best of your ability. Writing is not a contest. There will always be people who write better or worse than you do. Your goal is to write clear, logical prose and produce it in a timely fashion. That's it. Of course, if you are a gifted writer, it can only be to your advantage. But, as I said earlier, writing is like a muscle—the more you use it, the stronger it will get.

If you adopt the "good enough" principle, you will be able to undertake projects—and succeed at them—you otherwise might only have dreamed of. When I was starting out in my first job as an academic librarian, our director sent around an e-mail announcing a Fulbright opportunity in Morocco. It was a three-week assignment that would require the applicant to lecture daily in French or Arabic on interlibrary loan, cataloging and acquisitions. Although I knew nothing about interlibrary loan and just the basics of cataloging, and acquisitions, I applied for the position knowing that my research skills were strong enough to do the preparation necessary for this assignment and to do an acceptable job. I had studied French in college, but I thought that with some review I would remember enough of the language to get by. And if it wasn't good enough, I always could ask for help once I got there. This was shortly before the Second Gulf War. To my surprise, I was chosen for this position, most likely because I was the only applicant. I gave workshops on all aspects of technical services. The librarians at the institute pitched in when I had trouble expressing myself in French. Everyone was satisfied, and I was relieved. My expectations were not high. My goal was to do the best job I was capable of, and I did. I also had the adventure of working and traveling in North Africa.

RULE #2 BEFORE YOU START WRITING, ASK YOURSELF, WHAT DO I HOPE TO GAIN FROM THIS PROJECT?

The second rule of professional writing involves looking ahead to the future. Before you start any writing project, think about what you'd like to gain from the experience. Let's say you're serving on a library search committee. Your primary objective is to put together a job advertisement that will attract the most qualified people possible for the position. But you might have decided that soon you too will be looking for a new job. There is nothing more eye opening than being on a search committee and critiquing the candidates to give you a sense of how to conduct yourself in an interview. As you review job applications, you might decide to keep a copy of those cover letters that really stood out, while at the same noticing which letters the committee discarded. (See examples of both of these on pages 118 of this book). You probably have realized that those letters that looked and sounded the least professional were the ones in which the applicants weren't under consideration and that the ones that did not address the responsibilities of the job being advertised were summarily discarded.

A similar example involves a librarian I know who is particularly adept at getting internal grants from her institution. When I asked her what her secret was, she said she had been lucky enough to sit on her university's grant review committee in the past. When her term on the committee ended, she had kept a few of the successful applications. Because she understood what the committee wanted, she was able to tailor her proposal accordingly. This included strategies like asking for a smaller award and applying for modest funding from another philanthropic institution to make up the difference.

Was she taking advantage of the situation? I don't think so. My colleague worked very hard on the committee; however, she also took the opportunity to learn firsthand what made a winning grant application. Are you writing to establish yourself as an expert in the field? To learn about an area you want to become familiar with? Join a committee that shares your interests. Volunteer at your institution to work on a project that will teach you practical skills you need to acquire.

RULE #3 TAKE ADVANTAGE OF WRITING CONVENTIONS

The three basic documents used in professional writing are the letter, the memo, and the report. The letter is used for correspondence, the memo for administrative or legal matters, and the report for documentation. The last thing you should be doing when you start a writing project is to reinvent one of these standard document types. This book is full of examples you can use to inform your own work. Take advantage of them.

Writing conventions have been in place since the first professional writers came into existence several thousand years ago. They were known as scribes. Whether they used ideograms, pictograms or an abstract writing system like Arabic, their role was to record information that couldn't be entrusted to memory. They transcribed letters, conducted legal business, and documented transactions using a proscribed formula—similar to what we refer to as a "template" in this book.

Did you know that George Washington considered Alexander Hamilton too valuable to fight the British because he was Washington's scribe, so to speak? Like the scribe, you can use established conventions to help you write professionally. Focus on the content of your message. There is no need to reinvent structures that already exist.

RULE #4 REPURPOSE YOUR RESEARCH

Writing is not a one-shot deal. Research you've done, ideas that you may only have begun to explore, and questions that others have raised about your work can all be developed further. Take a look at anything you've written professionally, such as a newsletter, report, or library blog, and see whether it can be repurposed. The same holds true for conference presentations and poster sessions. I have a colleague, a literature professor, who is well-known for her productivity. Although she has written on a number of different topics, most of them have grown out of the research she has done for her earlier publications. If she finds information that does not fit into one project, she carefully files it away for future use. If you are a librarian, you are being paid for your ability to find information. If this skill is valuable to others, it is valuable to you. Save information you couldn't use and see if you can repurpose it in a future writing assignment.

RULE #5 WORK STRATEGICALLY

It is very easy to start writing and hope that everything falls into place as you go along. In reality it is much less work if you can do as much preplanning as possible. This means stopping to consider what resources you'll need, what kind of time constraints you are working under, and what challenges you might meet along the way. Preplanning is tied closely to project management. At the administrative level, library project management usually involves coordinating the actions of a team that has been tasked with gathering information, often with the purpose of initiating institutional change. This may be at a directive from higher administration or dictated by events that are taking place within the library itself. Perhaps there has been a significant increase of tweens and teens coming to the library in the afternoon, and your director has decided that resources need to be reallocated and additional programs set up. Would you be able to do a brainstorming activity to get this project going? How would it look drawn on paper?

Let's take a look at a LIS student's project planning list for a paper on public library management. This strategic way of approaching a writing project should serve you well as you transition into the library profession.

Choose four public libraries within a 20-minute area from home to visit
Check library homepage and town sites for library statistics and census data
Make appointment to interview library directors
Do a literature search for keywords "public libraries" and "library management"
Read sources and create a rough bibliography
Finalize questions for directors
Conduct interviews
Begin paper outline

Now, imagine that you are a public librarian who writes the monthly blog for the town library. Although the lists they create are different, both the MLIS student and the professional librarian are going through the same kind of mental processes.

Scan local, regional, national, and professional news sources for ideas
Decide on a topic
Look for additional background sources
Decide on key points to discuss
Create a rough outline of the blog
Begin first draft

GETTING STARTED WITH THIS BOOK

The book contains 9 chapters devoted to a different issue involving professional writing. Each chapter includes examples of the topics under discussion, accompanied by questions for you to consider. These examples and questions are reproduced in The Workbook, which is found in the Appendix.

You will want to keep a notebook for writing down comments and ideas. Maintaining a notebook not only helps organize your thoughts, it will also train you to be more observant. This is particularly important if you are an academic librarian or a LIS professor and need to develop a research agenda. But it also is just a good habit to get into. Too often during the course of the day we see or hear something that might be useful to the work we do and quickly forget about it. Writing these thoughts down may spark all sorts of ideas for projects in the future.

In order to get the most out of this book, you'll need the following:

1. A notebook to store your ideas. This can range from an old-fashioned notebook to an app for your smart phone.

2. A calendar or calendaring system to keep track of the due dates of all your writing projects. Products you might try are Google Calendar, Microsoft Outlook and Meekan, which works with Slack.

3. Folders (print or electronic) to store your documents.

4. Some kind of writing implement—a tablet, an iPad, pen and paper— whatever you prefer using.

5. Access to a citation program like Endnote, Zotero, Noodle tools and/ or a style manual. In the case of library and information studies, the citation style generally used is APA.

The best way to learn is by doing, and it is recommended that you complete the exercises found at the end of the book in the Workbook. The exercises are meant to reinforce the topics covered in each chapter. There is also a section at the back that contains templates that you can refer to.

CHAPTER TAKEAWAY

In this chapter, we stated the cardinal rules of professional writing: start with a game plan; borrow, don't recreate material that already exists from scratch; remember that your goal is to write clearly, not to write well; and determine how a writing assignment can benefit you as well as your employer, your professor, or tenure and promotion committee. These goals don't have to be mutually exclusive. If you can grow as a librarian, you are a more valuable asset to your workplace.

NOTE

1. University of Virginia Library, Charlottesville, VA. "University of Virginia Library Annual Report 2014." August 13, 2018. https://static.lib .virginia.edu/files/AR2014_web.pdf.

TWO

The Basics of Writing

You may be surprised to learn that not only is our spoken language con-
stantly changing, but our literary language is too, albeit more slowly. You
can tell that the first is true simply by watching an old black-and-white
movie and listening to the way the actors talked. You can do the same with
written language, by comparing texts taken from different time periods and
observing their stylistic differences. The three examples below are from
1890, 1941, and 2017, respectively. All have something to do with libraries.

The first passage is taken from the *Autobiography of Andrew Carnegie*.
Carnegie was a wealthy industrialist and philanthropist who helped finance
the building of public libraries across the United States at the turn of the
20th century. He is largely responsible for the public library movement in
this country.

EXCERPT FROM THE AUTOBIOGRAPHY OF ANDREW CARNEGIE

I resolved to begin at once my first web. True enough, the gods sent thread in the
proper form. Dr. J.S. Billings, of the New York Public Libraries, came as their agent,
and of dollars, five and a quarter millions went at one stroke for sixty-eight branch
libraries, promised for New York City. Twenty more libraries for Brooklyn followed.
My father, as I have stated, had been one of the five pioneers in Dunfermline who
combined and gave access to their few books to their less fortunate neighbors. I had
followed in his footsteps by giving my native town a library—its foundation stone laid
by my mother—so that this public library was really my first gift. It was followed by
giving a public library and hall to Allegheny City—our first home in America.[1]

The second passage is from a 1942 issue of *College & Research Libraries* devoted to the war effort. In December 1941, the Japanese attacked Pearl Harbor and the United States entered the Second World War.

EXCERPT FROM THE UNIVERSITY LIBRARY AND THE WAR[2]

THE UNIVERSITY LIBRARY and the war—what part can it play in the rapidly changing scene?—that is a question of deepest concern to us all. We have been swept off our feet by the sudden impact of war. What can we do to contribute? How be a part of the war effort? How justify our existence? We have the urge to accomplish great things, to do more than we have ever done before, something dramatic, unusual, spectacular. We have talked much and written at length on the morale, democracy, the library in national defense. Most of us have formed definite opinions as to what our place should be.

It seems to me that our greatest contribution to the war is to continue business as usual. One of the qualities of the British that we have admired most is their ability to go on with their daily tasks maintaining as nearly normal a trend of life as is possible in the face of desperate obstacles. The university is the great educative body. The library is its hand-maiden.

Lastly, here is a passage from a 2017 article that appeared in *International Information and Library Review.*[3] It discusses the inroads Google has made into public primary school education.

EXCERPT FROM "DEVICE-DRIVEN RESEARCH"

The use of a technological device as the main method for research changes the student experience in significant ways. Perhaps the most important phenomenon I have observed is an endless loop of "search and click" behavior among students when searching for information. A variety of research has pointed out the dopamine release that can occur when gaming, checking email or clicking on internet links (Dokoupil, 2012). Many students find the activity of clicking and looking for information more satisfying than actually finding an article and reading it. It seems that the old reward of finding an answer to a question and reading it has been replaced by the reward of clicking a link and arriving somewhere interesting. Sensitive trackpads can lead to an accidental click on a link, resulting in a change in topic. Faster and faster wireless internet access, and voice command services like Siri shorten patience and raise expectations that students will get results immediately and effortlessly. These aspects make an impact on all researchers, it is important to note, regardless of age. Young students, still forming their habits of mind, however, are most vulnerable to the negative impact of the equipment.

Some of this language may seem old-fashioned or stilted to you. The reason for this is because our society—how we relate to each other, how we think, and how we speak—has changed over time. The three writers use very different rhetorical devices. Andrew Carnegie's allusion to the ancient Greek story of Theseus and the Minotaur ("I resolved to begin at once my first web. True enough, the gods sent thread in the proper form.") likely is not recognizable to most people today. Probably neither is the biblical reference from the second excerpt: "The University is the great educative body. The library is its hand-maiden." As far as the third, do you think 30 or 40 years from now people will be aware of the enormous influence Google had on education in the early 21st century? Or will Google's success be eclipsed by another information technology enterprise and its impact forgotten?

These observations should encourage you, especially if you have a tendency to be hard on yourself as a writer. There is no one right or wrong way to compose a text. Even if a particular style of writing is in vogue at a particular moment in time, a few years from now, tastes may change. Write clearly and simply. And remember the first rule of professional writing: your writing only need be "good enough."

THE ELEMENTS OF STYLE

The title of this chapter is *The Basics of Writing*, but the book's approach is heavily indebted to William Strunk and E. B. White's manual, *The Elements of Style*. *The Elements of Style* was first published in the United States in 1920 and is now in its fourth edition. This slim reference work has lasted so long because it explains the idiosyncrasies of the English language in an engaging and succinct manner. Although the book provides advice on grammar usage, spelling, and style, Strunk, who was a professor at Cornell, and White, a *New Yorker* staff reporter, knew that the vagaries of grammar and spelling have very little to do with good writing. They are simply conventions that have developed over time. The best thing to do is not to question why these conventions exist but instead make note of them and try to learn them. A good way is to say words out loud, triggering your aural memory. I also suggest that you buy some old-fashioned file cards and write down several times the correct form of words you have misspelled or misused. Writing by hand is one of those mysterious processes that enables the brain to establish a connection between previous and new knowledge. Substantial research also shows that writing by hand contributes to comprehension and memory retention. More importantly, it encourages the writer to process information slowly.

Errors in grammar and spelling are important to correct because they cast doubt on your professionalism as a librarian. After all, if you haven't bothered to check your own work, what other mistakes have you made? Luckily there are only a few rules to remember when it comes to grammar; spelling mistakes can largely be corrected by using spell-check, a good dictionary, and a thesaurus.

English, for example, is full of irregular verbs. In their present and past tenses "dig" and "sing" are conjugated as dig, dug, have dug and sing, sang, sung. "Walk" and "place" are conjugated as walk, walked, have walked and place, placed, have placed. The reason for this discrepancy lies in the historical past. All four of these verbs have Germanic roots and were originally spelled very differently—for example, sing is derived from the Old German word, *singan*.

If you are a native speaker, congratulations—since the end of the Second World War, English has been the language of international commerce. If English is not your first language, you may have some hurdles to get over. Chinese speakers, for example, do not have separate words for "male" and "female," which makes it difficult for them to recognize gender (he, she, him, her). Non-native speakers also have a difficult time understanding the role of articles (the, an, a, and so forth), as, in fact, do many people whose first language is English. If you know that there is a particular grammatical construction that you are unfamiliar with, ask someone to proofread your writing for you.

In spite of the difficulties of spelling and an inordinately rich vocabulary (English is a fusion of Old English, a Germanic language, and French, a Romance language), there are advantages to writing in English. Its sentence structure is very simple—most often the syntax of a sentence is constructed in the form of subject–verb–object. Short, simple sentences are preferable to long, complex ones. Most speakers can get by with a relatively small vocabulary, since the grammar is so easy to learn.

There are seven rules particular to the English language that I'd ask you to focus your attention on and, if possible, memorize.

RULE #1 **HOMOPHONES**

Homophones are words that sound alike but have different meanings. Two good examples are "effect" and "affect." Effect is derived from the Latin word, *efficere*, or to bring about or accomplish. Affect is from the

Latin word *affectare,* to show preference for, to be inclined to, or to have affection for. Because these words entered our language from Latin, they have kept intact their meaning and spelling; their pronunciation, however, gradually became one and the same.

A partial list of homophones that you should master are:

advice	advise
complement	compliment
effect	affect
elicit	illicit
emergence	immergence
fare	fair
foreword	forward
hole	whole
holy	wholly
stationary	stationery
principle	principal
proceed	precede
waiver	waver

RULE #2   IRREGULAR PLURAL NOUNS

Most plurals of nouns are formed by adding "s," if the word ends in a consonant or a vowel, or "es," if it ends in "s" (tables vs. the Joneses). There are, however, words borrowed from Latin or ancient Greek that have retained the same spelling in the plural that they had in the original. Naturally, a plural noun also takes a plural verb. Some words, like "agenda," are often used to signify both single and plural nouns. The correct form, "agendum," is rarely used in colloquial speech.

Singular	Plural
Agendum	Agenda
Criterion	Criteria
Focus	Foci
Phenomenon	Phenomena

RULE #3 THE APOSTROPHE

The apostrophe is used for two purposes: to indicate possession (e.g., Mary's ball, John's toy) and to indicate that two words have been elided together (e.g., it's, there's, can't).

That is why "its" (possessive) is spelled without an apostrophe, and "it's" (it is) is spelled with an apostrophe. Common words that have a contraction or elision include "let's" (let us); "don't" (do not), and "can't" (cannot).

RULE #4 CAPITALIZATION

The rules for capitalization are fairly simple. The names of people (John Johnson), honorifics (Dr., Ms., and Mr.), book titles, and place names are capitalized. The first letter of a sentence is always capitalized.

RULE #5 GENDER

There has been a trend over the over the last 20 years to replace "he" with the gender-neutral "they" in cases where the noun signifies a general, rather than specific, person. In the past the word "one" was used to signify a gender-neutral pronoun. I personally prefer to vary the pronouns he and she. But by all means follow modern usage. An easy compromise is to make the noun preceding the personal pronoun "they" plural as well.

RULE #6 COMMON MISSPELLINGS AND THE FAULTY CONJUGATION OF VERBS

A few words are commonly misspelled or, in the case of verbs, are incorrectly conjugated. These words, for whatever reason, seem to jump off the page at the reader. Just take note of them, so they don't creep into your own writing.

Receive instead of recieve

"Lay" (to place) is declined lay, laid, have laid

"Lie" (lie down) is declined lie, lay, lain

"Lie" (to not tell the truth) is declined lie, lied, have lied

"Drag" is declined as drag, dragged, have dragged (although drag, drug, drugged is often used as a colloquial form in the Midwest)

Don't confuse "loose" with "lose"

Don't confuse "proceed" with "precede"

Don't confuse "than" with "then"

RULE #7 THE PERSONAL PRONOUN

The personal pronouns, me, myself, and I, are difficult to get right because they are often mixed up in colloquial speech. Some examples of correct usage include the following:

I am not myself today.

He gave me a friendly nod.

Jim and I went to town.

Try saying the sentence, "He gave the book to you and me," which is correct and then say, "He gave the book to you and I." If you are inclined to use "I" as an indirect object, repeat the first sentence, "He gave the book to you and me," a few times until it sounds right. You can also drop the "you and" part of these sentences to see if they sound right (e.g., "He gave the book to I" won't sound as natural as "He gave the book to me."

DIFFERENT KINDS OF LANGUAGE

As we examine the various document types that constitute professional writing, you will find yourself becoming an expert at recognizing the distinctive linguistic features of each: the legalistic language used in a request for proposal (RFP), the bureaucratic language of a memo, and the colloquial language of a blog posting. This does not mean that any of these are examples of "good" writing—in fact, the author's writing style might seem repetitive or pedestrian to you. Stock phrases and clichés are part of the formulaic approach that defines professional writing. This is because the purpose of professional writing differs from creative writing. In creative writing, the author is working with a very broad palette—the English language. Her job is to use language that sparkles and engages readers. In professional writing the goal is to help you easily comprehend what you are reading. That being said, the more you write, the more you will develop your own voice as a writer.

CONNECTING WITH YOUR AUDIENCE

The first rule of writing professionally is to use language your audience understands. This is not as easy as it sounds because the way we speak changes according to the circumstances we find ourselves in. Think of the conversations you have throughout the day—the words of prayer you use in your place of worship; the respectful tone with which you address a person in authority, such as a judge or a policeman; and the intimate vocabulary you use with your spouse or children. In some countries, there are actually more than one kind of language. Russian, for example, has words used only for philosophical and religious topics (a high language) and a separate vernacular for everyday matters (a low language).

No author writes for people in the abstract; he writes for individuals in the particular. Are your audience members part of the newcomers' club, needing information about services and programs, or are they representatives from an accreditation body who need access to last year's annual report? Obviously, their needs are different. Who are you writing for? Librarians? Patrons? Donors? Publishers? Professors? Funding Agencies? Most likely, you would address each of these groups differently.

Depending on its familiarity with the topic, your audience may only partially understand what you are trying to communicate. If you use language that is specific to our profession, make sure your audience is familiar with it as well. Phrases like "librarians, who participated in the pilot project, reviewed forms of authority control, including VIAF and WorldCat identities, before beginning BIBFRAME training" might be a sensible choice for an internal document but confusing if your report is intended for a more general audience.

By way of an anecdote, several years ago, a public library director invited a well-known primatologist from the local college to talk to the Friends of the Library about her field research in Uganda. The Friends had come expecting a colorful slide show of the scientist's life in the mountains, but instead the topic was so esoteric and specialized that the committee members came away feeling confused and talked down to. Don't let this happen to you. Know who your audience is and pitch your message accordingly.

LANGUAGE CUES

One of the ways that we make sense of what we read is by recognizing prompts in a text. These may be words that are part of a field's professional vocabulary, or they may be abstract ideas that encompass concrete processes, such as terms like "digital literacy" or "emerging technology." Your mind processes these metaphors or figures of speech as semantic cues that alert you to what the discussion is about.

Librarianship contains many words that would baffle people outside our field (e.g., ILS, metadata, reference query, granularity, or interlibrary loan). Yet these words form the basis of our professional conversation. Other fields also have vocabulary that is specific to their discipline.

Let's look at two examples. One is taken from a peer-reviewed journal in the field of Slavic studies; the other is from an OCLC white paper. See if you can spot the differences and similarities between them.

> The second category of response to the question "What is verse?" would point to the evident "patterning" of language in verse, patterning above and beyond what would be expected in practical language. Generally such patterning is perceived in terms of recurrences of prosodic features such as dynamic stress, intonational pitch, or temporal pause, or in terms of organization of euphonic features, as in assonance and rhyme. The repetition of grammatical (morphological) and syntactic structures likewise occurs in some poetries as the dominant aspect of patterning. . . .[4]

> The library profession may consider developing IR [institutional repository] copyright clearance "best practices" in order to supplement and augment existing copyright directories. This would not only advance our current permissions clearance and IR deposit practices, but, because we would be actively and systematically seeking permissions, it would have a greater impact on the availability of open access scholarship, and could provide an opportunity to further engage authors in this issue.[5]

Did you notice that the authors used specific words as a kind of shorthand to represent key concepts? Which excerpt was easier to understand? If you picked the second, was it because you were already familiar with the underlying concepts the writer was referring to?

Many academics write in the passive voice. Because their intended audience is other academics, scholars want their work to sound formal and abstract. By switching from the active to the passive voice, the subject is immediately disambiguated from the rest of the sentence. Take for the example this sentence in the active voice, "I saw my brother," and compare it with this sentence in the passive voice, "My brother was seen by me."

An overuse of the passive voice is frowned on in librarianship, as it is in many other disciplines of praxis. In the second excerpt we just looked at, almost all the sentences are in the active voice and the author of this OCLC white paper has made an effort to keep the sentences as simple as possible. This is one of the major differences between academic and professional writing.

OBSERVATIONS ON STYLE AND COMPOSITION

In this book, I try to get away from thinking about writing as either a creative act or one that requires an extensive knowledge of grammar and spelling. Instead I stress an approach that is based on imitating existing structures (the template method). However, there are genres, such as the critical essay or the editorial, whose success depends on the quality of the writing. These pieces are often beautifully crafted and use narrative devices, such as alliteration, parallelism, and repetition, to draw attention to the authors' key points. Although we no longer copy out examples of prose or poetry in order to learn how to write rhetorically, we can still observe and benefit from good writing.

The example below is taken from Michael Gorman's book *Our Enduring Values Revisited: Librarianship in an Ever-Changing World.*[6] This excerpt is framed as a polemic, which means that the author is arguing for a particular point of view.

> We must begin with the basic premise that everyone has a right to have access to library resources and services, irrespective of who they are and where and under which conditions they live. That concept is known as equity of access. Equity does not mean equality, but it does mean fairness. It is a key element in the concept of social justice—the idea that every person in society is entitled to a fair shake. In a world in which social justice prevailed, there would be no barriers to the elementary rights to which we are all entitled. In such a society all would have equal access to library resources and services as well as the universal rights to justice, medical care, employment, education, housing, free speech, and liberty that all humans have irrespective of their status and condition of life. We inhabit a far from an ideal world, and the things that distinguish us each from the other have an effect on our use of libraries as they do on every other service that we need or want. An ideal world of equality of access is out of reach, but it is by no means impossible to achieve a world in which librarians and library users have reached a far greater state of fairness than now. Equity of access is often referred to as "unfettered access." "To fetter" means "to restrain or confine"—a metaphorical extension of the notion of physically shackling or fettering a human being. The metaphor is continued in the phrase "unfettered access"—that is, access to libraries and their services that is unconstrained and free.

Gorman has a particularly interesting style of writing. He literally builds his argument through what he asserts are statements of fact. The paragraph in fact is so tightly structured that the reader will find it very difficult to break apart Gorman's argument. Also notice the repetition of emotionally charged words that he uses, such as equity, justice, and equality.

THE NARRATIVE STRUCTURE

The most basic narrative structure consists of three parts—an introduction, the body of the text and a conclusion. The introduction informs the reader of the topic, the body of the text presents the author's thesis, and the conclusion summarizes what has been stated. This gives the reader three opportunities to understand what the document is about.

A template of the Chicago Public Library's About Us page, www.chipublib.org/about-us, might look something like this—a simple narrative structure and stylistic devices, both making this a good example of professional writing:

Structure	Stylistic Devices
Introduction	Short sentences
Body of Text	Active verbs/present tense
Conclusion	Heightened language

SUGGESTIONS ON HOW TO MAKE YOUR WRITING STRONGER

Remember that grammar and spelling rules that apply to one language usually don't carry over to another. Neither do aspects of style. A good example is German, which, although similar to English, is an inflected language whose word order is just the opposite of ours (the verb generally comes at the end of the sentence, whereas in English, the verb comes directly after the subject).

In English, the sentence is the basic unit of writing. These sentences can be combined into paragraphs, which in turn create a linear narrative. Even if initially you find that the development of your thesis is a bit choppy, you can easily correct that by treating paragraphs as flexible packets of information that can be moved throughout the text until the writer is satisfied.

Now let's take look at a completely different method of constructing an argument: the use of transitional words to create a bridge from one idea to another. Note how the author relies on these transitional words to describe, list, and contrast how different libraries view collection development.

Collection development, a functional area common to most libraries, often takes on different forms depending on the type of library in which a collection is being developed. For example, the staff at a central academic library often views collection development somewhat differently than does the staff at a departmental library supporting individual academic units such as the business school. Yet both units—the central academic library and the departmental business library—encounter similar challenges in collection development, but not always at the same time or with the same group of users. These challenges are similar enough that both library units can learn from one another; collection development programs and policies that have been developed in one unit can be applied in the other. A brief comparison of these issues can be made and parallels between the two types of libraries can be drawn by exploring some of the factors impacting library collections today—external pressures on physical space, questions about collection size, the debate over licensing versus purchasing digital information, and the increasing need to make resources available to remote users. Central academic libraries as well as academic business libraries have encountered some of these factors to varying degrees and the efforts of each type of library to work through these factors may influence the work of the other type.[7]

Okay, so now you're satisfied that you have worked out an appropriate plan, conducted comprehensive research, and written an adequate draft; what is more, you've checked your grammar, punctuation, and spelling for acceptable usage. Everything seems to be all right, yet. . . . As you reread your paper, what immediately hits you is that it's dull, but more so, it doesn't develop the point you think is most important in such a way that it is most important. The corroborating details are accurate, yet. . . . If you're almost asleep, so will your reader be. The casualty of dull writing is your message. You failed to communicate with the urgency, or significance or vitality that you had wanted to give your writing.

What can you do? There are several ways of approaching your problem that will make the writing stronger, more meaningful, and more appropriate to your topic. Here are two of them that you might try.

Revise the original with an eye to sharpening language usage, that is, say what you mean in a clear way. Avoid such generalized terms as "something," or any of its relatives ("anything" and the like), and such overused judgmental terms as "amazing," "different," and "awful." Make those adjectives work for you to reveal distinctions. If it shines, is it "radiant," "resplendent," or "shimmering"? Or something else? (Oops. See how "something" can work, too.) Purge your writing of "I think," "I believe," "I know that. . . ." That you are writing your report or blog shows that. But, as important as word usage is, word elimination has its value too. Be careful not to overwrite. Omit unnecessary words. Do not repeat or restate anything unless you're developing or transitioning an idea. Next, try enriching your verbs as they will drive your argument. Use verbs that present a viewpoint other than the state of being, and be sure you're using the appropriate tense. Think of words to enhance, enliven, or even to electrify your topic, if that is your intention. Think about the specific role you're assigning the idea and use the language that reveals that. Don't hesitate to use dictionaries to help you. Try a few versions.

Reconsider your sentence structure. If you find you want to highlight something, write a short simple sentence (e.g., God loves you.) and its contrast (e.g., War is hell!). Now you can develop your thesis. If you want to balance or construct a parallel, be simple by using a compound sentence: "Give me liberty or give me death." These short versions give clear focus to what will follow. To continue energizing your paper, use all of the forms of sentence structure that work best—simple, complex, complex-compound, compound. This variety will help the reader to engage in your discussion with more ease. Along with varying the kinds and lengths of sentences, try beginning them with a single word, such as, "Luckily, Shakespeare left us many plays and ideas to think about." Try beginning with a phrase, such as "In the long run, it was easy to repair," and an independent clause, such as, "Notice that this makes the reader alert to what follows." In other words (phrase), vary your sentence structure and sense to emphasis the points that advance your topic.

Chrysanthy Grieco,
Emerita Professor of English,
Department of English, Seton Hall University

Let's look at a paragraph taken from Christine Borgman's book, *From Gutenberg to the Global Information Structure*,[8] which does much the same thing. The text is held together using two different techniques. The first is through transitional words. The second is through conjunctions that establish a series of compare and contrast arguments.

The more intertwined tasks and activities become, the more difficult it becomes to isolate any one task for the study. In the past, most theory and research presumed that the human activities involved in access to information could be isolated sufficiently to be studied independently. This is particularly true of information-seeking behavior, a process often viewed as beginning when a person recognizes the need for information and ending when the person acquires some information resources that address the need. Such a narrow view of the process of seeking information simplifies the conduct of research. For example, information seekers' activities can be studied from the time they log onto an information retrieval system until they log off with results in hand.

The process can be continued further by following subsequent activities to determine which resources discovered online were used, how and for what purpose. Another approach is to constrain the scope of study to library-based information seeking. People can be interviewed when they first enter a library building to identify their needs as they understood them at that time. Researchers can follow users around the building (with permission of course) and can interview the users again before departure to determine what they learned or accomplished.

DISTANCE YOURSELF FROM YOUR WRITING

To be able to dissociate yourself from your work is one of the most important lessons you can learn as a writer. The process of writing can be incredibly seductive. Instead of focusing on a particular turn of phrase or sentence you admire, try to view your writing through the eyes of your reader. If you wonder whether your ideas make sense, find colleagues or family members and explain to them what you are trying to say. If they find something unclear, chances are your readers will, too.

COMMONALITIES WITH GRAPHIC DESIGN

Among other conventions are typographic conventions, including headings, bullets, and the use of paragraphs, fonts, and line spacing that help people visually make sense of what they are reading through the process of chunking, or breaking down a text into smaller pieces of information. Words also alert readers to what is important—active verbs like "increase" and "decrease" and transitional words like "because," "therefore," and "as a result." The same is true for the use of specialized vocabulary, such as the superlatives "high achiever" or "energetic professional" that are found in job advertisements.

Let's take a look at some conventions of graphic design. Just as we saw with our examples from social media, design elements tend to function in similar ways in print and electronic media. A Web designer, for example, uses font size and color to direct viewer to the most important elements on the page. A writer does the same thing by using a hierarchical structure like a table of contents and appendices to organize his or her work.

The close relationship between the written word and graphic images has to do with the way writing began, as pictographs. These images gradually developed into abstract symbols called graphemes, which we refer to as letters of the alphabet. Printing—the medium which sparked the universal advance of reading—took these letters and standardized them, through the use of common typefaces. Since the invention of the first Gothic font, thousands of typefaces have been developed—first for moveable type, then for larger mechanical printing presses, and finally for the computer.

Two kinds of fonts, serif and sans serif, are used. Serif fonts contain a serif or a flourish on the edges of the letters; sans serif fonts are plainer. Sans serif fonts are generally regarded as being easier to read online and constitute the majority of digital typefaces. The reverse is true for print, which favors serif fonts.

Theoretically, each typeface should evoke a different emotional response in the reader. Designers often pick a particular font (the various manifestations of a certain alphabet type) because of its impact on how a viewer perceives and understands a text. The following sentences are set in Arial Plain, Arial Bold, and Arial Italic, respectively.

The lazy cow jumped over the fence.

The lazy cow jumped over the fence.

The lazy cow jumped over the fence.

Below are three typefaces commonly used in our profession: Times New Roman, Arial, and Century Gothic. These are shown below.

TIMES NEW ROMAN

The close relationship between the written word and graphic images has to do with the way writing began, as pictographs. These images gradually developed into abstract symbols called graphemes, which we refer to as letters of the alphabet. Printing—the medium which sparked the universal advance of reading—took these letters and standardized them, through the use of common typefaces. Since the invention of the first Gothic font, thousands of typefaces have been developed—first for moveable type, then for larger mechanical printing presses, and finally for the computer.

ARIAL BOLD

The close relationship between the written word and graphic images has to do with the way writing began, as pictographs.

These images gradually developed into abstract symbols called graphemes, which we refer to as letters of the alphabet. Printing—the medium which sparked the universal advance of reading—took these letters and standardized them, through the use of common typefaces. Since the invention of the first Gothic font, thousands of typefaces have been developed— first for moveable type, then for larger mechanical printing presses, and finally for the computer.

CENTURY GOTHIC

The close relationship between the written word and graphic images has to do with the way writing began, as pictographs. These images gradually developed into abstract symbols called graphemes, which we refer to as letters of the alphabet. Printing—the medium which sparked the universal advance of reading—took these letters and standardized them, through the use of common typefaces. Since the invention of the first Gothic font, thousands of typefaces have been developed—first for moveable type, then for larger mechanical printing presses, and finally for the computer.

Does one typeface resonate more than another with you? Your response may depend on your familiarity with a particular kind of font; for example, this book is printed using the digital version of Times New Roman. Other reactions may be more subliminal. If you love to cook, you may be drawn instinctively to the typeface, Sabon, which is often used to print cookbooks.

A second graphic design element that has carried over from print is the use of fixed spacing between lines and the creation of white spaces around the text. Generally, a writer will use double line spacing for paragraphs and single line spacing for lists, when creating a document in Word. Margins are generally 1.5 inches on each side.

The use of fixed line spacing changed the way text was presented. When the printing press was invented, it was no longer necessary to abbreviate words (as is done in Hebrew today or ancient Greek in the past) because of the difficulty and expense of writing on parchment or velum.

No matter what typeface you pick to write your text, most often the font is 11- or 12-point type. The text itself is either justified or has a ragged edge. Justified text looks like the pages of this book:

The close relationship between the written word and graphic images has to do with the way writing began, as pictographs. These images gradually developed into abstract symbols called graphemes, which we refer to as letters of the alphabet. Printing—the medium which sparked the universal advance of reading—took these letters and standardized them, through the use of common typefaces. Since the invention of the first Gothic font, thousands of typefaces have been developed—first for moveable type, then for larger mechanical printing presses, and finally for the computer.

And unjustified or text with a ragged edge looks like this:

The close relationship between the written word and graphic images has to do with the way writing began, as pictographs. These images gradually developed into abstract symbols called graphemes, which we refer to as letters of the alphabet. Printing—the medium which sparked the universal advance of reading—took these letters and standardized them, through the use of common typefaces. Since the invention of the first Gothic font, thousands of typefaces have been developed—first for moveable type, then for larger mechanical printing presses, and finally for the computer.

Justified text looks cleaner and more professional. Text that is unjustified tends to look much more casual and is often used for more informal documents like e-mails and letters.

CHAPTER TAKEAWAY

This chapter dealt with the mechanics of writing. I've only a few observations because I believe you already intuitively know the rules of grammar, syntax, and spelling. I encourage you to rely on your auditory memory to tell you what sounds right and to memorize the few rules and examples that don't come naturally. Presentation is always important in any kind of professional writing. When you are starting a project, make sure you choose a size and type of font that is commonly used at your work, or pick one that you feel will reinforce the topic you are writing on.

NOTES

1. A. Carnegie, *Autobiography of Andrew Carnegie* (New York: Sheba Blake Publishing, 2014). Retrieved from http://ebookcentral.proquest.com/lib/shuedu/detail.action?docID=1672581.

2. E. Christoffers, "The University Library and the War," *College & Research Libraries* 4, no. 1 (1942): 18–24. Retrieved from https://www.gutenberg.org/files/17976/17976-h/17976-h.htm.

3. K. Ahlfeld, "Device-Driven Research: The Impact of Chromebooks in American Schools," *International Information & Library Review* 49, no. 4 (2017).

4. H. Eagle, "Verse as a Semiotic System: Tynjanov, Jakobson, Mukařovský, Lotman Extended," *The Slavic and East European Journal* 25, no. 4 (1981): 47–61.

5. Ann Hanlon and Marisa Ramirez, "Asking for Permission: A Survey of Copyright Workflows for Institutional Repositories," *portal: Libraries and the Academy* 11, no. 2 (2011): 695–696.

6. M. Gorman, *Our Enduring Values Revisited: Librarianship in an Ever-Changing World* (Chicago: ALA, 2015), 99.

7. N. Rupp, "Learning from One Another: Collection Development in Central Academic and Academic Business Libraries," *Business Reference and in Academic Libraries Committee* 7, no. 1 (2012). Retrieved from http://www.ala.org/rusa/sections/brass/brasspubs/academicbrass/acadarchives/acadbrassv1n4/acadbrassv1n4a1.

8. C. L. Borgman, *From Gutenberg to the Global Information Infrastructure: Access to Information in the Networked World* (Cambridge, MA: MIT Press, 2003), 7.

THREE

The Writing Process

Often, a writer does not know exactly what he or she wants to say at the beginning of a large or multifaceted writing assignment. Rather than forcing yourself to immediately come up with a draft, try letting your mind wander. As ideas occur to you, write them down but don't evaluate them. This will come at a later point. This phase of exploration is often referred to as prewriting. You should be familiar with this method if you've worked as a school or instructional librarian. It is often the first technique students learn when doing research. Prewriting can take a variety of forms and it may be helpful to try one of the methods suggested below.

Prewriting is the critical foundation of the writing process; ensuring the product meets the desired goal. The temptation to dive right into creating a rough draft, shortchanging or avoiding prewriting, almost assuredly leads to lost time and missteps. The oft quoted phrase, "proper planning and preparation prevents poor performance," reflects how essential pre-thinking and prewriting are to success (Keague, 2012).

Developing a successful prewrite begins with identifying your audience and the expected content. This information provides you with parameters for what information must be included and what is nonessential. The next step includes selecting an appropriate organizational strategy to frame your ideas and connections. There are numerous prewriting strategies, such as developing questions, outlining, free writing, bullet point lists, story boards, brainstorming, and mind maps to name a few. No single strategy is best, and you might find that you need to combine a few in order to frame your thinking for the drafting phase. A tip about what strategy to begin with: ask yourself how you approach a problem. If you are a linear thinker, you might start with outlining, whereas if you are a global thinker, you might start with a mind map.

How might prewriting be applied to something like report writing? One approach begins with brainstorming: writing down all of your ideas and questions about the topic, followed by reflection on which of the items address the audience and content expectations, and removing those that are extraneous. A second strategy, creating a mind map, expands on the brainstorming by allowing you to visualize the identified key concepts and establishing connections between them. This may be done by hand or by using a Web-based tool, many of which are free. For some, the mind map provides enough of a fleshed-out framework to begin the drafting phase. For others, a third strategy could be applied by creating an outline from the mind map to sequence the content and connections. This example illustrates the framing and refinement of your ideas, the desired goal of prewriting, to prepare you for phase two of the writing process, drafting.

Keague, S. *The Little Red Handbook of Public Speaking and Presenting.* CreateSpace Independent Publishing Platform, 2012.

Grace May, Associate Professor,
Department of Educational Studies,
School of Education, Hall University

MIND MAP

A mind map is essentially a sketch or diagram that shows the relationship among similar ideas. For example, you and several colleagues might have been asked to prepare a report on the upcoming children's room renovation at the library. Your initial mind map might show a loose association between green design, a multipurpose space, a display of children's art projects, and a reading nook.

You can buy a sophisticated spreadsheet program or simply jot down your ideas on a napkin or a piece of paper. You might look at IDEO, a program created by the Chicago Public Library and the Aarhus Public Library, which is financed by the Bill and Melinda Gates Foundation. IDEO promotes a concept called "Design Thinking for Libraries," which encourages actions like brainstorming, roleplaying, and collaboration.

Another similar prewriting tool is a concept map. Like a mind map, a concept map consists of a central idea that is placed within a hierarchy of other ideas. Often the facilitator of library workshop may jot down ideas on a large piece of paper taped to an easel or wall, and participants may be asked to add their suggestions. This serves the same purpose as a mind map or a concept map.

GROUPING YOUR IDEAS

At this junction, you may find that you have too many ideas, and you might want to think about eliminating some that seem impractical or not material to your main focus. Or you might find that some of your ideas are very similar, and they should be grouped together. Whatever you decide, now is the time to turn three or four of your ideas into concept headings. These headings will serve as the basis of your document.

AN OUTLINE

Some of you probably remember writing essays in high school using file cards. Your teacher instructed you to write a topic sentence on each card and put your supporting documentation underneath. The idea was that if you could organize your ideas as an abbreviated narrative, it would make writing much simpler. In many ways, the approach is similar to that of a template. The difference is that an outline requires you to commit to a narrative structure before you have even begun to write. The template method encourages you to see paragraphs as the building blocks of prose and to move them around until they read as a narrative.

Using an outline is a good choice if you are working on a complex document like a planning document. You might begin by creating a concept map and then develop an outline that looked something like this.

I.   **Introduction**
     A.
     B.
II. **Body of the Report**
     A.
     B.
     C.
     D.
III. **Conclusions**

You'll notice that at this point the outline is quite minimal. As you do research, you will need to flesh out the document. The introduction might in its next phase look something like this

I. Introduction

    A. Purpose of planning document

        1. Why now?

        2. Goals?

        3. Etc.

    B. Previous planning documents

        1. 2016

        2. 2017

        3. Etc.

A BULLETED LIST

Writers who are more visual in their approach may want to try a bulleted list, which consists of brief points or topics to be covered. I find that a bulleted list allows you to think in a more fluid way than outline. You may have an annual review coming up, and you want to prepare points of discussion both for your meeting and the written report you will prepare. The result might look something like this:

- What have I accomplished this year?
- How does it differ from last year?
- What do I need to emphasize?
- What are my goals for next year?

STORYBOARDING

A storyboard consists of a series of drawings that tell a story. Originally, storyboards were used as visual aids to help a director keep a film on track. They can be very useful for individuals who respond visually to information. School librarians sometimes will use digital storytelling to present online lesson plans to students. This is a form of storyboarding as well.

A GANTT REPORT OR AN ACTIVITY REPORT

Before you start writing, you probably will want to document the activities you'll need to undertake and put them in chronological order with a due date beside each one. As you gain more experience, you probably will be able to do this by relying on knowledge you've gleaned from previous projects. Some writers advocate using a tool called an activity report. An activity report allows you to organize and plot your activities against a timeline. A popular activity report is a Gantt chart. You can download many versions of Gantt charts from the Web or create one yourself using Excel.

THE FIRST DRAFT

In Chapter 4, I advocate writers use a process of composition I call the "template method." I'll refer to it many times throughout the book. The template method means that you begin by identifying what kind of writing you are doing. Are you working on a report? A memo? A master's thesis? Once you have determined this, the next step is to find a piece of writing you can use as a model. You will discover as you read through this book that most professional writing only differs in its content; you could look, for example, at a hundred CVs, and you would see that they all follow the same formula.

If you are starting the first draft of an essay, identify what kind of thesis you intend to develop (these can be found in Chapter 10). For example, you may be writing a compare and contrast essay that begins with an introduction, contrasts two different points of view, and ends with a conclusion. Don't worry too much about how your prose sounds at this point. It is much more important that that you are developing a thesis that clearly has a beginning, middle, and end.

THE SECOND AND THIRD DRAFT

Once you've finished the first draft, you probably would do well to set it aside for a few days. This will give you time to distance yourself from your writing. Now read the first and last sentence of each paragraph consecutively to make sure your thesis is making sense. If not, rearrange the paragraphs until they do. Remember that paragraphs, not sentences, are the building blocks of any lengthy piece of writing, and you should feel confident moving them around to see if they would fit better in another section of the document. You'll want to proofread your document to make sure it has no spelling or other errors and that your citation style, if the document requires citations, is correct.

GETTING RID OF BAD HABITS

All of us have idiosyncrasies that prevent us from producing our best work. Some of these practices serve us well in other areas of our life. Procrastination, for example, is a personality trait that is an asset in some professions, like journalism, because a reporter intentionally leaves a story unfinished until shortly before his or her deadline is due. This way he or she is sure to include the most recent information available. Procrastination can be a useful strategy for individuals who respond well to working under pressure and is often the method of choice for college students and academics who are writing to meet a deadline. For someone who doesn't have self-discipline, however, it can be disastrous.

The perfectionist is a personality type similar to the procrastinator. This driven individual has unrealistically high expectations of what he or she can accomplish. The perfectionist cannot distinguish between projects that merit her genuine attention and those that can be accomplished with a minimum of effort. Like the procrastinator, she tends to get discouraged and often gives up before completing a project.

Two other personality types you might recognize are the disorganized writer and the multitasker. The first individual is similar to the procrastinator, except that he or she is hopelessly disorganized. This lack of organization is often a sign of creativity—you'll sometimes see an office that looks like a whirlwind, but its occupant can put a hand on whatever he needs at a moment's notice. This not true of the disorganized writer who tries to postpone the inevitable as long as possible and uses the disorderliness of his or her working space as an excuse not to begin.

The multitasker on the other hand has the opposite problem. This person is ambitious and task-oriented, but because he or she is juggling so many projects, he or she doesn't have a firm grasp on any of them. In meetings, he or she either is texting or catching up on e-mail.

Unconsciously or not, each of these four personality types is operating from the assumption that he or she will not be successful at writing. It's a huge psychological burden to carry. These unproductive behaviors have their roots in childhood, when students come to realize that their academic worth is being judged almost entirely through written assignments. This is the start of a growing dislike and fear of having to write. It's unfortunate because being a proficient writer is one of the most useful assets for building a successful professional career.

Bad habits are exactly that—repetitive actions that served a purpose at one time but now just get in the way of what you want to accomplish. If you recognize yourself in one of these personality types or have other habits that are preventing you from achieving your goals as a writer, acknowledge them, write them down in your journal, and then for good measure cross these entries out. This is because the good news is you can break bad habits by replacing them with another kind of behavior.

A RESPONSE TO THE PERFECTIONIST

Perfectionists see writing as a reflection of their self-worth. If you recognize yourself in this description, stop and take several deep breaths. Remember the first rule is that your writing only needs to be good enough. If you can see your writing through that lens, it will make it easier for you to edit your work. Try to clear your mind of any kind of emotional attachment you have to the assignment you are working on. Now go back and look at the document as objectively as you can. What are its strengths? Its weaknesses? Is there a beautifully turned phrase you are admiring that does not fit with your thesis? If so, eliminate it. Do the paragraphs follow in a logical order? If not, reorganize them.

A RESPONSE TO THE PROCRASTINATOR

The procrastinator like the perfectionist is emotionally invested in his or her work. He or she is so afraid of failing that if he or she misses a deadline, he or she may actually be relieved. Notice that I've used the word "failing," as opposed to "failure," because failing implies a deliberate action on the part of an individual. Now there is no way his or her work can be rejected or ridiculed. If you identify with this personality type, try to think of a situation in which this behavior might be to your advantage. Some people find it easier to write in one burst of effort. This only works, however, if all the preparatory work has been completed in advance. Another method is to select a template before you start your research. The simple act of doing this should help scale back your anxiety. You are no longer invested in "your" writing—it has become instead a boilerplate document to complete. Examples of simple templates can be found in the latter half of the book and in your workbook.

A RESPONSE TO THE DISORGANIZED WRITER

If you fit into this category, you will need to take a hard look at your organizational skills. First, ask yourself why your workspace is in such disarray. If you can get at the source of the problem, you probably can fix it. Perhaps you are rebelling against the way you were taught to write in school. You may have been required to use notecards or create an outline. Or you may have been told that you needed to demonstrate that you had a thesis statement before starting to write. These lessons were probably frustrating and nonproductive. While we are advocating using a template for professional writing, we know that in the beginning (creative) stages of composition, people do better if they are encouraged to use methods that spark their imagination, such as mind maps, which allow individuals to think in a circular rather than linear fashion.

It makes sense to keep track of your activities through some sort of filing system. This could be done on your computer or simply by using an old-fashioned accordion file, with the contents of each file labeled. These can be separated out by job responsibilities, committee work, publications—whatever makes sense to you. I have a big basket under my desk where I toss memos, reports, and anything else that has relevance to my job position. I go through the basket at the end of the year to jog my memory about what I've accomplished. After I've written my annual report, I toss the contents of the basket and start afresh for the year. How much effort should you spend on organizing your material? It all depends how detail oriented you are. More important is to set up a filing system you feel comfortable with and assiduously add to it throughout the year. This way, you'll have everything in place when you need it.

Dedicate an afternoon to the decluttering your workspace. The most obvious solution is to go through and sort your papers, discarding those you don't need. If you don't want to create a filing system, you can keep them on piles on the floor. The idea is to have at hand the material, so you don't have to waste time searching for it.

A RESPONSE TO THE MULTITASKER

It's a genuine question as to whether individuals are able to multitask, that is, perform several tasks simultaneously. An example of this is reading e-mail while listening to music and writing a paper. Whether multitasking is indeed possible or not, the most important takeaway is that however many projects you are involved in, they must finish within a time frame and be completed independently.

You might want to change other habits. For example, if you have trouble focusing, try changing when you do your writing. Most people are aware of their own biorhythms. If you are a morning person, working on the library's newsletter in the late afternoon makes absolutely no sense. It would be much better to change your routine and start early in the day when you are the most productive, even if this requires some readjustment of your schedule at work.

HOW DO YOU LIKE TO WORK?

This leads me to my next point: How do you like to work? The stereotypical image of a writer sitting down at a desk every day at the same time to work for one or two hours is only one of the ways you can approach a writing assignment. It's just as probable that you might want to work for five or six hours on a Friday, when things are slow at the library, or organize your work into half hour increments every morning. While the first method requires self-discipline, the second mainly relies on good time-management skills. Maybe you grew up like I did, doing homework alongside a sibling at the kitchen table. This kind of writing feels far more comfortable to me than sitting at a lonely desk in an office. Or you might need total silence in order to concentrate. In that case, close the door of your office or find a nook in a quiet area of the library to write.

Any piece of writing can seem overwhelming, and it may appear difficult to know where to begin. One way is to start by tackling the easiest parts of a project first, and leaving the most difficult ones for later. You might write the introduction last instead of letting it determine the direction of the rest of your thesis or do the bibliography first to reacquaint yourself with your sources. Or you may want to divide your writing project up into sections and approach them sequentially. Another way is to organize your tasks in order of the time needed to accomplish them. In this approach, you would accomplish those tasks that are the simplest to do when you have a free moment at work, and you would block out larger amounts of time for those that require more concentration. Whichever method you choose, you want to keep track of what you are doing. Your planning system can take the form of a spreadsheet, like those provided by Google or Excel, or a simple handwritten list.

You might be asked by your library director to do an interview with the local historian for your town's centennial. Your schedule might look something like this:

Project	Interview John Duffy, town historian. Podcast will be released the day before the town celebration and available through library homepage and blog
Due dates	Interview takes place by May 3rd Editing completed June 1st Uploaded to library Web site June 6th
Tasks completed Still to do	✓ Finished questions research for interview ✓ Picked location for interview Interview, editing still needs to be done Ask Duffy for photos. Copyright clearance? Advertise in library newsletter
Notes	Duffy available a.m.; remember to print out questions

WRITER'S BLOCK

Like perfectionism, writer's block is a condition that can cripple writers. Everyone has experienced it at some time, but hopefully, for you, the professional writer, it will never impact your work as it does the creative writer. If you are having trouble putting words down on paper, change your approach to how you measure your productivity. Instead of using time as a measurement, write to a word count. Generally, 250 words equals one written page; 3,000 to 6,000 words constitutes 12 to 24 pages. Once you identify the word count of your piece, it makes writing far easier. You are now working toward reaching a numerical goal. If you write 250 words on Monday, you have completed between one-twelfth and one-twenty-fourth of a typical article or report; if you write 500 words on Saturday, you have completed one-fourth to one-eighth of your work. Don't worry if in the process of writing, your organizational structure changes. That's par for the course. Most professional documents keep to within a standard page range. For example, an average report is somewhere between 20 and 40 pages, depending on the subject matter. A cover letter is generally one to one and one-half pages. A personal recommendation is one to three pages.

Let's take as an example a report that needs to be approximately 25-pages long. Since we know the total number of pages, we can assign a rough page count to each section: a one-page abstract, a two-page introduction, a 16-page main section, a two-page conclusion, and a two-page works cited list. But you might feel that the introduction is too short or that the main section should be broken into four parts, instead of one. Whatever you decide, it is much easier to adjust your document now rather than later. You will also find it a good way to break through writer's block. Your next task is to complete one section at a time, regardless of how long it takes. Anyone can write three pages in a sitting. It doesn't matter if you are dissatisfied with what you've written. If you keep at it, you will eventually have a first draft to work from.

Let's take another example, the term paper, which constitutes a large part of a student's grade. Before beginning to write, the student needs to know the paper's requirements—its length, the citation style the professor has requested, and other information that most likely is laid out in the syllabus. If a graduate student is expected to write a 20-page paper and turns in three pages in the form of rhyming couplets, he or she will automatically fail. If a student turns in a paper that contains citations done in MLA, when the professor has requested APA, he or she most likely will get marked down a grade.

Below is a page breakdown for a 20-page term paper. I've deliberately left the page count for each section blank. Can you fill them in?

SECTION	PAGE NUMBER
Abstract	
Introduction	
Survey of the literature	
Body of text	
Implications for future research	
Concluding remarks	
Works cited	

WHAT IF YOUR WRITING IS REJECTED?

Sometimes, even when you've done extensive research and preparation, your writing is not accepted, or it is accepted under the condition that you do revisions. This may be a departmental report for your library, a paper for your teacher, or an article for a peer-reviewed journal. The best thing you can do is try to disassociate yourself emotionally from the situation. You can ask yourself if there is merit to the criticism and if so make revisions. If you believe the criticism is too vague, you can ask what needs to be done to make the document acceptable. Sometimes, you can avoid finding yourself in this situation by asking a colleague or friend to read your work in advance, or you could go directly to the person who will be receiving the document and ask for comments and suggestions midway through. Under no circumstances should you argue with your critic and defend what you've written. Everyone is entitled to his or her opinion.

CHAPTER TAKEAWAY

Perhaps all you need to be a more effective writer is to modify your habits. It makes no sense for you to write early in the morning if you are a night owl; likewise, there is no reason to work in a crowded and noisy room if you need quiet in order to concentrate. The most important thing is to acknowledge what is stopping you from doing the kind of work you'd like to accomplish and to fix it. This is where using a template can prove particularly valuable. It will allow you to emotionally distance yourself from your prose, which is often a problem for writers without much experience. If you are a procrastinator, using the template method should help you organize and complete a writing assignment quickly and efficiently. And if you are perfectionist, this method you should also help you move to distance yourself from your prose.

FOUR

The Template Method

Over the course of my career, I've adopted a technique I call the "template method." The template method is based on the observation that professional communications—memos, reports, newsletters, and the like—are written according to a standardized formula, and if you understand what that formula is, you can reproduce it. This chapter will cover two types of templates: the basic template and the customizable template.

If you look up the original meaning of template in the *Oxford English Dictionary*, you will find that it is "an instrument used as a gauge or guide in bringing any piece of work to the desired shape; usually a flat piece of wood or metal having one edge shaped to correspond to the outline of the finished work." This is a good metaphor for professional writing. Professional writing is a craft. It becomes easier to do over time as you gain experience. However, just as with any craft, writing doesn't come automatically. You will need to continue to hone and shape a text until you are satisfied with the result. And remember, the more you practice, the better you will become as a writer.

A BASIC TEMPLATE FOR A DOCUMENT STRUCTURED AS A NARRATIVE

The introduction
The main body of text
The conclusion

This template consists of only three parts: a beginning, middle, and an end. It may seem simplistic, but this is in fact the underlying structure of every narrative form, no matter how complex the storyline. It is a structure that we human beings seem to have an affinity for because it corresponds to our notion of how events unfold over time. If your document is a narrative and does not contain a three-part structure (i.e., a beginning, middle, and end), you need to determine if any of the sections need to be expanded or new ones added. Good examples of this are library reports, graduate term papers, and journal articles.

A BASIC TEMPLATE FOR A CV OR RÉSUMÉ

Another kind of basic template is the curriculum vitae (CV) or résumé. The template for both these can be expressed as the following;

Name
Address
Contact information
Education
Work experience
Technology skills
Volunteer work
Personal recommendations

One final example is the recommendation letter. The template for this can be expressed as the following:

Date
Salutation
Name of individual being recommended
Body of text
Point 1
Point 2
Point 3
Close
Name/title of reference

You'll find other, increasingly complex examples as you progress through the book; however, a narrative, CV and recommendation letter are three types of templates you will use over and over.

WHY CHOOSE THE TEMPLATE METHOD?

Using a template to lay down the initial structure of a text is not a new idea. In medieval and Renaissance Europe, it was common for students to model their writing on the works of ancient Greek and Roman authors. Much of this literature was poetry. Within this literary genre were different subgenres: the epic, the ode, and the pastoral, for example. Each had a fixed metrical pattern, imagery, and a common subject matter, which made them easy to imitate. A student could prove his mastery of a genre by creating a new composition that thematically and stylistically resembled an earlier classical work. The highest praise was reserved for students who were able to write "in the style" of a great master, such as Vergil or Ovid.

This approach to teaching writing is different from the method we use today in the United States. Children in kindergarten and first grade are taught the basic rules of composition first—in particular spelling—before doing any writing at all. This makes sense because in English many words are not pronounced phonetically. To learn how to read, you first have to learn the spelling rules that will enable you to sound out the text. Later, as children gain more confidence, they begin to express their own ideas by writing short sentences.

This method of teaching reading and writing is relatively recent in the United States. In the 19th century, it was customary for students to memorize inspirational works like the Gettysburg Address and to copy passages out as a way to reinforce their comprehension and improve their writing skills. As with medieval education, the emphasis was on learning by imitating a master rhetorician or writer. An appreciation of the power of spoken language has continued in some communities today, most notably in the African American community. In recent history, for example, two political figures, who were also well-known orators, modeled their speeches on the writings of earlier great statesmen. Martin Luther King Jr. was inspired by Mahatma Gandhi, and Barack Obama was inspired by Abraham Lincoln. Other prominent political figures have been able to use language to gather supporters behind them. Winston Churchill changed the course of the Second World War through his impassioned speeches to Parliament, as did Franklin D. Roosevelt through his Fireside Chats.

You might try this as one way of freeing yourself from the limits of your current approach to writing. Instead of worrying about grammar and spelling, listen to recordings of speakers you admire and try to hear what makes their speeches successful. Generally, you will find their success is due to the use of stylistic devices, such as alliteration, repetition, and parallelism.

Take one of our most famous American speeches, Abraham Lincoln's Gettysburg Address, which was delivered at Soldiers' National Cemetery just outside Gettysburg, Pennsylvania, a few months after the famous battle there. Let's see if we can find the structure of this document.

Four score and seven years ago our fathers brought forth on this continent, a new nation, conceived in Liberty, and dedicated to the proposition that all men are created equal.

Now we are engaged in a great civil war, testing whether that nation, or any nation so conceived and so dedicated, can long endure. We are met on a great battle-field of that war. We have come to dedicate a portion of that field, as a final resting place for those who here gave their lives that that nation might live. It is altogether fitting and proper that we should do this.

But, in a larger sense, we cannot dedicate—we cannot consecrate—we cannot hallow—this ground. The brave men, living and dead, who struggled here, have consecrated it, far above our poor power to add or detract. The world will little note, nor long remember what we say here, but it can never forget what they did here. It is for us the living, rather, to be dedicated here to the unfinished work which they who fought here have thus far so nobly advanced. It is rather for us to be here dedicated to the great task remaining before us—that from these honored dead we take increased devotion to that cause for which they gave the last full measure of devotion—that we here highly resolve that these dead shall not have died in vain—that this nation, under God, shall have a new birth of freedom—and that government of the people, by the people, for the people, shall not perish from the earth.[1]

You'll notice that the address is quite short, only three paragraphs long. If you examine it closely, you will see the text is organized as a timeline. The first paragraph refers to the founding of the United States, the second describes the battlefield where Lincoln was standing, and the third expresses the hope that good will come out of the tragedy of the Civil War. In preparing our own speech, we could model our efforts on Lincoln's and create a template that looks something like this:

> Events in the past
> The effect of past events on the present
> The effects of present events on the future

The template we just created might be used to celebrate a graduation or as a wedding toast.

THE THREE-STEP METHOD

There are only three steps to the template method:

1. Choose the right template for your writing assignment, either a generic template or an existing document similar to your own.

2. If you are working from a generic template, make any changes necessary to reflect your own content. If you are using a preexisting document, you also will want to decide which sections of the text you can keep and which you need to customize.

3. Do the legwork required to make the document your own. This might involve doing research, making phone calls, or doing interviews. Once you've collected your information, you can add it to the appropriate section of the template. This will end up being the first draft of your document.

You will notice that, thus far, you haven't done any writing at all. This is intentional. In the template method, how you write is less important than how you organize your text. Remember, our ultimate goal is to create a document that is straightforward and easy to read.

A CUSTOMIZED TEMPLATE

We've mentioned two types of templates: basic templates, which are the equivalent of an outline, and customizable templates, which are preexisting documents that you can use as a model for your own work. Here is an example of an announcement that a search for a university provost is underway. Let's see if we can modify it to serve as a customized template for another, similar search.

ANNOUNCEMENT OF A PROVOST SEARCH

From: The Office of the President

The provost/executive vice president search was officially launched on November 30 with ads placed in the *Chronicle of Higher Education* and a number of other publications. The provost/executive vice president profile can be accessed on the school Web site.

The committee, working with search firm X, is planning to begin review of applicants for the position toward the end of January, with the expectation of interviewing semifinalists later in February.

If you know an outstanding candidate who might be interested in the provost/executive vice president position, please consider encouraging that person to contact us.

We will continue to keep you informed.

The Office of the President

We can use this communication as a template for the library's announcement to the community about the ongoing search for a dean of university libraries. Our announcement might look something like this:

To: The Community
From: The Office of Human Resources

A search for the new dean of the university libraries began on March 20th. Ads were placed in the *Chronicle of Higher Education*, the ALA Job List, and other relevant publications. The full ad has been posted on the Human Resources page at the university Web site.

The committee, working with search firm X, is planning to begin a review of applicants for the position at the end of April. Semifinalists will be brought to campus in June for interviews.

If you know an outstanding candidate who might be interested in the position of dean of the university libraries, please encourage that candidate to apply directly through Human Resources.

Sincerely,
The Office of Human Resources

Let's look at another template, this time for a fund-raising letter[2] that the American Library Association (ALA) makes available for free use. What kind of audience is this letter intended for? How do you know?

Dear (Community Business):

We need your help! The (Library Name) Library is offering a summer library program to the children of our community to encourage them to read for pleasure during the summer and to retain their reading skills. This year's theme is Dig into Reading.

To add to the fun and to create a sense of challenge that will keep kids reading, we'd like to offer incentives and contest prizes at various times during the summer. Because of our limited budget, we cannot afford to offer this without help.

We appreciate any donation you care to make. Possible donations include items to give away as prizes, small toys, coupons for free goods or services (admission tickets, fast-food coupons, free film, film processing), or cash to buy prizes to offer as a Grand Prize. We will mention the assistance you have generously donated in our publicity.

If you can help us in any way, please contact me at the library (phone number). We hope to include you in our summer plans. Many thanks!

Sincerely,
XXXX

This is a good time to discuss the difference between taking the example provided by the ALA and using it as part of a local fundraising appeal and appropriating a published document that you intend to circulate beyond your library. Using someone else's work that you intend to publish or use as a public document is an entirely different matter and can involve issues of copyright. You need to be very sure that you have not inadvertently appropriated someone else's work. Do a good job tracking your citations and always be sure to check your sources. However, don't worry that you are breaking some kind of rule or doing something nefarious by consulting the work of others before beginning your own. Plagiarism involves using the words of another, without giving proper attribution, not the structure of a text. And remember, a template cannot be copyrighted.

A SECOND CUSTOMIZED TEMPLATE

Let's say that you have just completed your first year as the head of a technical services department at a small college library, and you have been tasked to write the unit's annual report. When you ask your director what to include, she tells you to focus on significant achievements, goals, and priorities. But there is a problem. Because the library has recently relocated into a new space, you don't have access to previous files. Or you might have access to these reports but decide that they don't capture the full scope of your department's activities. We discussed in the previous chapter how you never should undertake any writing assignment without being clear about your purpose. Putting together this report should give an accurate snapshot of the strengths and weaknesses of the department as well as your own.

GETTING STARTED

Below is a template for a library annual report. Even though the template is meant to address the activities of the whole library, let's see if we can adapt in such a way that it will enable you to create your own departmental report.

LIBRARY ANNUAL REPORT TEMPLATE

Library's goals and objectives for the previous year
Departmental reports
Individual staff achievements
Library budget allocation
Usage statistics
Upcoming goals for the next year

Now you'll want to make the template your own. Feel free to eliminate any of the components that are not appropriate to your own situation. Your personalized template might look something like this:

Departmental goals and objectives—written by you with staff input
Reports of team leaders—written by acquisitions, cataloging, and metadata staff
Individual staff achievements—contributed by staff
Department statistics—assembled by copy cataloging, rare book cataloging, bindery, acquisitions, and check in staff
Upcoming goals for the next year—written by you

That wasn't difficult, was it? You've just created the start of your own departmental report!

You might only tweak the template below if you are a reference or instructional librarian whose job responsibilities remain the same from year to year:

Social Sciences Librarian
Annual Report FY 2016–2017
Teaching
Conducted 56 research consultations for History, Political Science, and Diplomacy undergraduates, graduates, faculty, and deans.
Taught 34 classes for English and University Life (15) and History, Diplomacy, and Political Science (19).
Research Guides had 4,676 views, up 22 percent from 2015–16
Liaison Work
Attended Political Science faculty meeting to ensure faculty had current understanding of databases and mapping tools to support digital and spatial literacy.
Conducted Hein Online Webinar for Political Science and Diplomacy departments.
Created and deployed outreach plans for liaison departments, including creation of Research Guides, publicity, and training for new databases, data sets, and research tools.
Served as project manager for PolicyMap (GIS mapping tool) and coordinated with departments to track program growth and faculty needs to support spatial literacy. Political Science, the Masters in Health Administration, and Anthropology participated.
Participated in Duplicates Project to ensure duplicate books were offered and delivered to liaison department.
Served on planning team Summer Digital Humanities Program with committee chairs; secured speakers for three-day program and was program presenter.
Presentations
Presented poster on Spatial Literacy at National 2017 Conference.
Committees
National Conference Poster Sessions Committee, 2015–present
Public Services Committee, 2016–present
Student Learning Outcomes Task Force
Member of the Digital Humanities Committee, 2014–present
Member of Collection Development Committee, 2015–present
Library Data Analysis Committee statistics
Education
Completed three courses toward MPA degree.
Completed Certificate (18 Credits), Graduate Program in Data Analysis.
Inducted into Pi Alpha Honor Society (3.7 GPA or higher, current GPA 3.8).

FORM FOLLOWS FUNCTION

Louis Sullivan, an American architect at the turn of the last century, is credited with coining the phrase "form follows function." By this he meant that how an object is used determines its design. Sullivan was speaking about architectural design; however, his statement applies to professional writing as well.

If you don't believe me, try this exercise. Close your eyes and imagine that someone has placed three documents in front of you. You are told that one of the items is your library's annual report, another is a meeting agenda, and the last is a performance review. One document consists of a thick stack of paper. Running your fingers along the edges, you can tell that the paper is of good quality that it has been professionally bound. As you flip through it, you estimate that it is a good 50 to 75 pages long. Another document has only a single sheet of paper, and the last consists of four pieces of paper. It shouldn't take more than few seconds to identify which document is an annual report, which is an agenda for a meeting, and which is a performance review.

This is because you already are familiar with one of the most important conventions of a professional document: its length. Length doesn't reflect how significant a document is, but it does signal what kind of information the document contains. For example, an annual report is a lengthy document that describes the library's activities during the previous year. An agenda is no more than a page long because it is a list of the order in which topics will be discussed by a committee. A performance review summarizes the activities of an employee over a year's period and shouldn't be more than a few pages.

Characteristics that are indicative of a specific document type are found not just in our own professional writing but in all genres of writing. Take for example, a formulaic narrative like the detective story. If you are a mystery buff, you know that every detective story begins with an unsolved crime and that authors, if they are any good at their craft, will provide a series of clues to help you, the reader, unravel the crime as you progress through the book. Detective novels are one of the most satisfactory and, at the same time, most formulaic kind of fiction writing. If the story ended without the author revealing the person responsible for the crime, it wouldn't be a detective novel, would it? If you go to the movies expecting a thriller, and find out that the film is actually a romantic comedy, wouldn't you'd feel cheated?

Writing that is built on a formula is called a "genre." Film, literature, and music are genres that belong to the creative arts, and mystery, romance, and sci-fi novels are genres of fiction. Even though genre is a term most often used in the humanities, it is a good metaphor for the different kinds of writing we do as professionals. Genres are organized according to a general classification scheme known as a "typology." Typology is a construct that is used in many different academic fields, among them anthropology, religion, and statistics. Our definition classifies kinds of professional writing according to their structural characteristics.

One of the advantages of the template system is that it is organized as a hierarchy, a classification scheme that librarians are familiar with. At the top of the pyramid is "professional writing." This category is divided into three parts—memos, reports, and letters. And beneath that are various document types: annual reports, meeting agendas, request for proposals (RFPs), and so forth.

Memos, reports, and letters are the most basic forms of written human communication, and you'd be hard-pressed to find any library being able to function without them. Most other types of professional writing are derived from these three.

THE MEMO

"Memo" is an abbreviation of the word "memorandum," which comes from the Latin word, *memorare*, to remember. Memos or memoranda serve the function of communicating information to the internal and external stakeholders of the library. Try to count the number of memos you receive during the day—these might include notices from your administration, Human Resources, or committees that you serve on.

Kinds of memos include memos to staff, administrators, and colleagues; memos of understanding, and meeting agendas/meeting minutes. Excerpts taken from a NIH policy memo, an MOU between a friends group and a public library, and Board of Trustee Minutes are shown below. They show the range of purposes a memo can take.

NIH PUBLIC ACCESS POLICY

This memo alerts you to an important new *federal requirement* contained in the Public Access Policy from NIH that will affect current and future NIH grants and contracts. . . . This policy becomes effective...

MOU BETWEEN A FRIENDS GROUP AND A PUBLIC LIBRARY[3]

The following will constitute an operating agreement between the Friends of the Anytown Public Library (Friends) and the Anytown Public Library (Library). It will stand until and unless it is modified by mutual agreement of the Friends executive board and the Anytown Public Library administration and minutes of the Board of Trustees of the Anytown Public Library.

BOARD OF TRUSTEE MINUTES

The spring meeting of the library's Board of Trustees was held on May 24th in the reading room. Under discussion was the upcoming bond issue for the library's new extension. The library director spoke, as did the project architect. It was resolved that the board would again meet within the next month, at which time the library director would present an update on the project. The following trustees were present. . . .

THE REPORT

Reports are the second genre of communication most frequently used in our profession. "Report" comes from the Latin word *reportare* [to carry back]. Reports are used to inform library decision making and to disseminate information to the public and to the library administration and staff. Unlike the memo, which is often short and to the point, the report is lengthy and evidence based.

Kinds of reports include committee reports, departmental reports, and institutional reports, and newsletters. An excerpt of the State of America's Libraries Report 2017 is included below:[4]

School libraries serve 98,460 of our nation's public and private schools. More than 90 percent of traditional public schools report having a library, while 49 percent of private charter schools report having one. These libraries have always supported the curriculum, encouraged student creativity, and promoted lifelong learning. Today's challenges—such as information literacy, intolerance, and funding cuts—highlight the need for well-funded school libraries and credentialed school librarians.

School librarians use standards-based learning experiences that promote critical evaluation of print and digital resources and the creation of valid student work. There is some evidence that school library budgets may be increasing, after five years of reductions, and there is hope that the Every Student Succeeds Act (ESSA) will be used in support of school libraries. The law includes language that allows schools to budget funds for school libraries and acknowledges school librarians as specialized instructional support personnel.

THE LETTER

The last genre of communication is the letter. A letter has all sorts of functions, but it is mainly used for correspondence. The word letter comes from the Latin word *litera* [letter]. The letter is the oldest of the three forms of communication—the earliest example, a 14th-century BCE diplomatic correspondence, was found in Mesopotamia. Perhaps because of its ancient history, the letter is the only media that still survives in a handwritten form.

We can't predict how writing will evolve in the future, but we do know that these three genres of professional communication—the memo, the report, and the letter—will continue to be viable for a long time. You'd be hard-pressed to imagine how the day-to-day activities of your library could take place without them.

CHAPTER TAKEAWAY

Conventions alert readers to what kind of text they are reading and help them draw on previous knowledge in making sense of it. We have borrowed the term "genre" from literary theory to refer to the main kinds of professional documentation used in our profession: memos, reports, and letters. Every document type adheres to conventions specific to its own genre. Learning what these conventions are will make the professional writing you do easier.

NOTES

1. A. Lincoln, "Gettysburg Address," November 19, 1863, taken from http://voicesofdemocracy.umd.edu/lincoln-gettysburg-address-speech -text/.

2. Children Summer Reading Sample Donation Letter. Available at http://tsla.libguides.com/c.php?g=784156&p=5616924.

3. Template for sample operating agreement. Available at www.ala.org /united/sites/ala.org.united/.../friends/.../sample-operating-agreement.doc.

4. American Library Association. "State of America's Libraries Report 2017." Available at http://www.ala.org/news/state-americas-libraries-report-2017.

FIVE

Born Digital

You may have noticed that, so far, I have not mentioned documents that were "born digital." Social media, like Facebook, Twitter, and blogs are still so new that few protocols or standards have developed for their use. Sometimes, as in the case of Instagram and Twitter, it is difficult to know whether these born-digital formats are simply new platforms for distributing content or new forms of professional communication. Eventually, protocols will develop for all digital media; however, until that time, most born-digital media are still derived from their antecedents in the analog world and follow similar rules of composition.

E-MAIL

E-mail is an example of a genuinely new kind of professional communication that is slowly starting to be codified. When first introduced in the 1990s, it resembled traditional correspondence—the honorific, name of the respondent, and the date were at the top of the e-mail. The text was organized in paragraphs, and the sender's credentials and signature appeared at the bottom. Today, e-mail has become the dominant form of professional communication, replacing the personal or business letter. It also is the most common form of communication in the academic community, so you need to learn how to use it, particularly if you are still in a master's program. However, it is only recently that protocols for writing e-mails have been established. Because of the informal nature of e-mail, it is easy to overstep the boundaries between professional and personal correspondence by using slang, acronyms, and emojis. When in doubt, err on the more formal side. This includes having a subject line that summarizes the purpose of your communication, a salutation, and traditional features (bullets, headings, and line spacing) to organize content. If you have never met or don't know your correspondent well, it is always better to address him or her by a title or honorific (Dr., Rev., Mr., or Ms.). A lawyer should be addressed as Mr. Mark Smith, Esq. An individual who has finished his doctorate, but who is not a teacher, could be addressed either as Dr. Mark Smith or Mr. Mark Smith, PhD.

One of the hardest things for librarians starting out in their careers to do is learn how to bridge the gap between communicating with their peers and communicating with individuals who are either older or who outrank them professionally. Because e-mail is still not a mature medium, it is easy to make a misstep. This dawned on me a few years ago when I arranged for Sarah, a work-study student at the library, to approach the director of a prestigious research institute about a summer internship. When the director hadn't gotten back to her in a few weeks, I asked Sarah to show me her e-mail. It began "Hi Mary, How's it going?" and rapidly went downhill from there. We rewrote the letter together, beginning with the opening salutation, "Dear Dr.," and I sent it off to the director with my own recommendation.

Below is an e-mail, announcing an upcoming workshop. The wording is simple enough that it can be used as a simple template. The invitation includes the dates, place, and Web site address. Because this announcement is intended for scholars, the e-mail frequently includes a common opening salutation (e.g., Dear, Colleagues, Friends) and a formal close (e.g., Best wishes, Truly Yours, Sincerely).

To our friends in the community,

Registration is now open for our "Master that!" computing workshops that will run from July 19th to the 23rd at the city library. Registration is due on July 1st. As last year, our program is being sponsored through a generous gift from Tony's Office Supplies and is free to all city residents. So come learn how to create a blog using WordPress, organize your digital files in Omeka, and try out our Makerspace. To find out more about this exciting program please go to our Web site.

The Library Tech Team

BLOGS

Blogging, like traditional print-based journalism, is text-driven. If the writing is good enough and the voice of the author strong enough, blogs have the power to change public opinion or policy, as they did in the on-the-ground coverage of the Arab Spring. They are similar to their antecedents, newspaper editorials and syndicated columns, but have a significant advantage: they can draw exponentially larger readership, sometimes numbering in the tens of millions, if they are posted on a commercial site.

Blogs often are used for marketing and promotion in libraries. Here is an excerpt from the blog *The Family Dinner Project*.[1] You could easily modify this blog to serve as a template for an announcement posted on a public library's blog.

GENERAL BLOG

On February 20, 2015, The Family Dinner Project partnered with Common Sense Education for a Community Dinner at the Waring School in Beverly, MA. The dinner was a time for parents, educators, and students to come together for a shared meal and meaningful conversations about social media usage, Internet habits and practicing good digital citizenship.

We asked participants in the event to share some of their thoughts with us and were struck by the overwhelming positivity we received in the comments. Many attendees reported that they have been continuing the conversations that were begun at the dinner in their own homes, while others say that the opportunity to experience a family dinner event has inspired them to try harder to bring their families together around the table more regularly.

INDIVIDUAL LIBRARIANS' BLOGS

This entry comes from Andromeda Yelton's personal blog, *across divided networks*. The blog comments on the intersection between feminism and technology. Because it is easy for individuals to self-publish blogs using an open-source Web platform like WordPress, the contents don't require mediation or a filter. Like many bloggers, Andromeda Yelton maintains a carefully curated homepage that includes her curriculum vitae (CV) and links to her professional presentations. Note the colloquial writing style and how Yelton gradually builds a case for women in tech.

Today I'm at a Wikipedia + libraries mini-conference, as a member of both worlds but also, strangely, neither. I write software for the Wikimedia Foundation (specifically the Wikipedia Library, which is among the conveners). I'm a librarian by training, and the President-Elect of LITA. But I also don't identify as a Wikipedian (my edit count is, last I checked, 5), I don't work in a library, and I have never worked in an academic library (whereas the other convener is the Association of Research Libraries).

This is a great excuse to be an observer and try out a tool that was going around Twitter a month ago: http://arementalkingtoomuch.com/.

It's a set of paired timers: "a dude" and "not a dude." You click the button that represents the speaker. At the end, you have a count of how much time each category held the floor. In our first session today, 52 percent of the speaking time was men.

Sounds equal! Except . . . 42 percent of the room appeared to be men. And as I looked around, I realized that all but perhaps one of the 10 men had spoken at least once, whereas about 5 of the 14 women had said nothing at all in our morning session. (Myself included; I was too busy processing the meta-meeting, tracking all of this.)

"Be bold," said the coffee mug in front of me. Who is bold?[2]

Jessica Olin curates *Letters to a Young Librarian*, a long-standing blog offering advice to librarians just starting out in their careers (http://letterstoayounglibrarian.blogspot.com). What makes Yelton and Olin's blogs effective is that they are well designed and frequently updated; most importantly, they provide readers with a free service (the authors' and contributors' expertise). These blogs establish both women as knowledgeable experts, while at the same time promoting their job qualifications and work background. Olin's blog has 2,948 followers on Twitter. In this excerpt from the June 8th entry of *Letters to a Young Librarian*, contributor Zoe Fisher discusses how to successfully participate as a team member in a library project. It can be used as a model for other essays on an individual librarian's blog.

HOW DOES THIS PROGRAM RELATE TO OUR GOALS (AS A DEPARTMENT, LIBRARY, ETC.)?

If you're in a new role, this question should help you get a sense of how your individual work aligns with your department and the library at large. What is the role of your department, and how does it work within the library? What is the library doing to improve and grow? With that in mind, how does your project help the library meet its goals? You want to know that your work matters to the organization, and the connection between your task and bigger goals should be clear.

What's at stake in this project? What would be the impact if this project *didn't* happen?

If you're being asked to do several things at once, this answer can help you prioritize. In most cases, a project with low stakes can be put on the back burner in favor of projects that have an immediate impact on your coworkers, your patrons, and library operations. But don't let a project with seemingly low stakes get you down—sometimes it can be difficult to see the big impact of a project until it's finished.

What do I already know that I'll be able to use in this project? Is there anything new that I need to learn or find out?

This is a good time to clarify what resources are needed in order to do this project. Do you need to call or e-mail someone you've never met? Use new software? Access files or materials you haven't used before? Hopefully there are some new things to learn in this project—that's the fun part![3]

LIBRARY BLOGS

Blogs serve a different function for an institution like a library. Like Twitter and Instagram, they are a medium used to attract a younger audience. The New York Public Library, which arguably has used blogging to the best advantage of any library, posted the following as its mission statement for blogging.

So in addition to being on-the-beat reporters, taking the pulse of events and activities around NYPL with up-to-the-moment coverage, think of our bloggers also as deep sea divers, swimming down, flashlights in hand, exploring the library's vastness and bringing knowledge to the surface.

Our aim is to develop the blog into the latest in a long tradition of librarian-generated genres designed to publish staff expertise and help users navigate the library's breathtaking array of collections and services. Like finding aids or research guides, NYPL blogs will be another powerful tool in our information arsenal.

Over time, the blog archive will grow into an enduring knowledge base, which we'll use to enhance and enrich the digital experience of the library. You'll find posts not only in Blogs, Videos & Publications (browsable by subject and channel) but peppered throughout the Library's website—supplementing search results and tied to relevant location pages, topics and events. The goal? Having the wisdom and expertise of NYPL librarians at your fingertips as you explore the site.

Please feel encouraged to engage directly with bloggers in the comment stream. To ensure a civil and focused discussion, comments will be held for a brief period before being published.[4]

In the entry below, the Tompkins Public Library uses its blog to promote a new writers group for teens. Notice that the library is offering virtual support for the group through its Web site, fully taking advantage of this medium.

TOMKINS LIBRARY BLOG

If you enjoy writing, please consider participating!! Although NaNoWriMo is an individual activity, the Falcon Writers group will be meeting in the library after school every Monday during November to write, discuss, edit, or talk about their novel for those that can attend. The Falcon Writers group also has a virtual classroom through the NaNoWriMo Young Writer's website that allows students to ask questions, chat about their novels, get advice, and more![5]

Twitter is a valuable social media tool. Careful curation of followed accounts and lists allows me to use Twitter for a variety of interests and goals. The variety of people who use Twitter facilitates connections with a more diverse group of people than I might otherwise connect with on a regular basis. The 140-character limit makes it easy to scan tweets quickly, similar to scanning newspaper headlines, for items of interest or relevance. I can follow experts, read or watch items they share links to, "listen" in on their conversations with others, and even join in if I choose. Hashtags allow me to follow conferences and events from a distance, as well as follow, or join in on, official Twitter chats or casual conversations on topics of interest. Twitter allows me to be part of a community where I can ask questions, share my work, share my knowledge by answering questions posted by others, and follow the work of my connections. Through Twitter I am regularly exposed to new ideas, new information, and new people helping me escape my echo chambers, as well as contributing toward my goal of lifelong learning.

Bobbi Newman
Community Engagement and Outreach Specialist
National Network of Libraries of Medicine

TWITTER

Twitter, as a medium, is similar to its antecedent, RFF feeds, the difference being that Twitter, as a Web-based platform, is interactive. It can contain embedded hyperlinks to other sites, as well as video and audio files. Generally, libraries use tweets to advertise new services, programs, and collection resources directed at a younger audience. A tweet is delivered directly to the subscriber's mailbox, which can be read and then reposted. This makes Twitter an incredibly fast messaging system. The New York Public Library, as of July 2017, had 275.611 followers on Facebook and 2,235,747 followers on Twitter.[6] Library of Congress (LOC) was one of the first organizations to realize the importance of collecting social media, and it began with Twitter feeds. As of 2013 LOC had archived over 170 billion tweets   (http://blogs.loc.gov/loc/2013/01/update-on-the-twitter-archive-at-the-library-of-congress). In the analog world, this would be similar to collecting letters and journal entries as primary source historical materials.

Twitter can be an effective tool for broadcasting professional announcements. See for example the American Library Association's campaign I Love Libraries (https://twitter.com/ILoveLibraries). Librarians have successfully used this medium to push information out to their followers (subscribers). Best practices include the use of a recognizable hashtag (e.g., #NYPL [New York Public Library] or #LOC [Library of Congress]). Hashtags are used in place of subject lines.

INSTAGRAM

Instagram, like Twitter, is a messaging service. On Instagram, subscribers can share photos, videos, and other visual media; they can edit and post material online; and like Twitter, they can classify their posts through hashtags. Libraries generally use Instagram to publicize events and displays. Because these posts are indexed through hashtags, a crowd-sourced, curated collection can be a powerful tool for libraries. Two Instagram collections that demonstrate this are #librarydisplay (http://www.instagram.com/explore/tags/librarydisplay/) and #bookfaceFriday (https://www.instagram.com/explore/tags/bookfacefriday/).[7]

YOUTUBE

YouTube is a Web-based audio and video hosting service used in our profession principally for instruction and the promotion of library services.

As with Twitter, YouTube is a communication platform and service rather than an emerging communication medium. For best practices on using YouTube in academic libraries, see Georgia State University's instructional video (https://www.youtube.com/watch?v=Pd0noUli1MQ) and IFLA's videos for libraries for children and young adults (https://www.youtube.com/playlist?list=PLNbNYMA4VlILn3XhaPuOkwlIpTY-0zHvq).

LIBGUIDES

LibGuides[8] is a content management system that enables librarians to present information drawn from catalogs, databases, and Web sites for their patrons in the form of a customized guide. What is interesting about this commercial product, which is heavily used by librarians, is that it allows librarians to create new content wrappers for information, a sign that perhaps LibGuides will eventually develop into a new document format.

OTHER FORMS OF THE DIGITAL

So far, we've talked about the social media tools librarians use to communicate with on the job, like e-mail, Facebook, and Twitter. But as in every other industry, librarians have been affected in a more visceral way by the digital revolution. These changes affect not only the work they do but also the research and scholarship they engage in.

CHANGING SCHOLARSHIP

For academic libraries, the most important event of the digital revolution was the shift from print to electronic journals at the beginning of the 21st century. The second most important event, and one that all libraries, not just academic ones are struggling with, is the shift from print books to e-books. After trying out several ideas, including a circulation model that resembled a physical library's checkout system, publishers have moved to a model in which chapters are disaggregated from their container, the book, and indexed individually in a database. Most likely the book, as we know it, will disappear, and users will be able to assemble a collection of materials and create a customized "book" on a topic of interest to them. There are other distribution models, like Demand-Driven Acquisitions (DDA) that does not require libraries to purchase books at all—rather, they are made available as MARC records in online library catalogs, e-books that can be activated for a fee. These developments affect libraries, of course, but they also affect the research agenda and publications of everyone involved in academia, including LIS faculty, academic librarians, LIS graduate students, and librarians who write as part of their ongoing research and praxis.

CHAPTER TAKEAWAY

Print documentation has been in existence for so long that the format is clearly established. This is not true of electronic communication like blogs, e-mail, and Twitter. These media are still developing, and it is not clear whether some of them are actually Web platforms rather than kinds of communication. Libraries have been early adapters of almost all new social media. One of the challenges for you, as a librarian at the intersection of information and technology, will be to see how far you can develop these new tools to advance the profession.

NOTES

1. Bri DeRose, "Bringing Common Sense to Media Use at Waring School," *The Family Dinner Project* (blog). April 22, 2015, https://thefam ilydinnerproject.org/blog/community-blog/bringing-common-sense-to -media-use-at-waring-school/.
2. A. Yelton, "Be Bold, Be Humble: Wikipedia, Libraries, and Who Spoke," *across divided networks* (blog), August 18, 2016, https://androme dayelton.com/2016/08/18/be-bold-be-humble-wikipedia-libraries-and -who-spoke/.
3. Z. Fisher, "What to Ask When You Are Given a New Project," *Letters to a Young Librarian* (blog), June 8, 2017, http://letterstoayounglibrarian .blogspot.com/2017/06/what-to-ask-when-youre-given-new.html.
4. "NYPL Blogs," *NY Public Library* (blog), n.d., https://www.nypl.org /voices/blogs/about-nypl-blogs.
5. "It's Time for NaNoWriMo," *The Book Nest* (blog), Tompkins HS Library, November 2, 2016, http://tompkinslibrary.edublogs.org/.
6. "Top 50 Librarian Blogs and Websites for Librarians," Library Blogs List, July 10, 2018, https://blog.feedspot.com/library_blogs/.
7. #librarydisplay, Instagram Community Web site, n.d., http://www .instagram.com/explore/tags/librarydisplay/.
8. "LibGuides Community," LibGuides Community, n.d., http://community .libguides.com/.

SIX

Shorter Documents

Let's start with the memo and move on to related document types, such as a memorandum of understanding, meeting minutes, and policy guidelines. *The Oxford English Dictionary* says the word memo first came into usage in 18th century England to describe a record being held for future reference in a court case. A memo can be any length, though most often it is quite short. In our profession, it is frequently used to report an administrative decision or to issue an institutional or departmental policy.

By now, you are probably starting to realize that the more structured a document is, the easier it is to use as a template. That is particularly true of the memo, which is one of the most formulaic kind of documents.

The first thing you'll notice about the memo below is how easy it is to identify. The inclusion of the recipient's name, title and address, the

---

A SIMPLE MEMO TEMPLATE

MEMORANDUM

To: Recipient's' name and job title
From: Writer's name and job title
Date: Current date
Subject: Description of what the memo is about

Messsage . . .

Salutation/Sign off
Writer's signature[1]

salutation, the body of the text, and the sender's coordinates alert you to the kind of document you are looking at.

Memos often are written in a kind of shorthand rather than in formal English. That is because memos are administrative directives. The memo shown below communicates a decision made by the college administration to allow retirees to keep their e-mail accounts.[2] Phrases like "retirees in other titles," "same naming conventions," and "excluded functions" show the resulting bureaucratization of language that can occur when a memo takes on this function. This communication serves as an official document (one of the hallmarks of a memo), the language is highly legalistic (another hallmark of an institutional announcement), and the format of the document is boilerplate. Most likely it was prepared by legal counsel.

What type of audience do you think the writer has in mind?

MEMORANDUM FROM AN OFFICE OF HUMAN RESOURCES

Subject: Retiree Email Guidelines

As you are aware, the University previously agreed to allow full-time teaching and nonteaching instructional staff represented by the PSC—as well as those in excluded functions and in the Executive Compensation Plan—who retired on or after September 1, 2013, to elect a retiree email account at the time of retirement, using the same naming conventions as the regular College email addresses, but with the addition of "**.ret**" to indicate retired. . . .

In the intervening period, a determination was made to allow all full-time teaching faculty and librarians to retain their regular College email addresses. . . . Retirees in other titles retain the option to request a "**.ret**" email account. . . .

This job posting describes what kind of library media specialist the Orchard Park School District is looking for, where the full advertisement is posted, and when interviews will take place. Because of its structure, the job posting falls squarely into the category of the memo.

JOB POSTING FOR A HIGH SCHOOL POSITION

The Orchard Park School District is looking for a dynamic person who is interested in moving our Senior High School library into the 21st century in terms of technology and collaboration with all teachers, but with emphasis on English, History, and Science teachers in the expansion of research projects. Orchard Park offers an attractive salary schedule and provides 5 years of service credit for salary placement. We will be participating in a Teacher

Recruitment Fair in the State Capital Convention Center on Saturday, March 15. The position is posted on our district Web site. Please contact humanresources@XXX.state.edu indicating your interest in our position. Interested applicants will submit their applications following the directions on the Web site. We will be scheduling interviews at the Teacher Recruitment Fair and in our district at a later time.

RESOLUTIONS

In academia, an elected body, such as a faculty senate, will occasionally present a resolution for its membership to endorse. Resolutions may be proposed for a number of reasons—in support or dissent of an action taken by the administration, or, as is the case of the example below, to acknowledge service or achievement by a member of the public library community. Note the formal language and organizational structure of this the resolution. Can you tell why a resolution is a variation of a generic memo?

A SIMPLE TEMPLATE FOR A RESOLUTION

WHEREAS
WHEREAS
NOW THEREFORE BE IT RESOLVED
ADOPTED THIS DAY

This is a simple resolution by library staff to honor an employee's years of service to the organization.

A RESOLUTION HONORING AN EMPLOYEE

Honoring XXX
WHEREAS, XXX has served as a Library Employee since December 1, 2000; AND
WHEREAS, her dedicated service and strong work ethic is exemplary; AND
WHEREAS, her strong organizational and supervisory skills enabled her Staff to grow stronger as Library Employees under her tutelage;

AND
WHEREAS, both her attention to detail and ability to see the big picture has helped to make the Library a better and stronger institution;
NOW, THEREFORE, BE IT RESOLVED
That on behalf of the Board of Trustees, The Staff, and the Library District, the Trustees hereby express gratitude and appreciation for XXX's 17 years of service to the Library and the Community.

Adopted this 21st day of December, in the year 2017.

A MEMORANDUM OF UNDERSTANDING

A related document is called a memorandum of understanding. This is an official, legally binding agreement between two parties. Memoranda of understanding are also referred to as "letters of intent." They memorialize a contractual agreement between two parties.

GIFT AGREEMENT

Name: _____ (Donor)
I irrevocably and unconditionally hereby donate and transfer to the Regents of the University of Michigan ("University") tangible personal property described in Attachment A (the "Donated Materials").

I understand and agree that disposition and use of the Donated Materials by the University will be at its discretion, in accordance with University policy and applicable law. Common uses include, but are not limited to, exhibition, display, digitization for preservation and access purposes, and making works available for research and scholarship.

I am transferring all rights, title, and interest in the physical Donated Materials. I hold none of the copyrights in the Donated Materials.

Modifications

I agree that any modifications to this Gift Agreement must be in writing and signed by me and the University.

Governance

I understand that the University will strive to use my gift for its intended purpose in accordance with University bylaws and policies, as well as applicable law. I understand that the University will administer my gift diligently in accordance with the requirements of this Gift Agreement, but if changes develop in the course of time, I understand that the University will use my gift as closely as possible to the purpose stated in this Gift Agreement, which shall be governed by Michigan Law.

Signatures

I represent and warrant that I am the owner of the Donated Materials described in this Gift Agreement; that I have full right, power, and authority to give, transfer, and/or license the Donated Materials as described herein; and that the information I have provided is accurate.

Donor Name: _____

Address: _____

Email Address: _____

Phone: _____

Signature: _____

Date of Donation: _____

The University accepts the gift and transfer of the Donated Materials in accordance with this Gift Agreement.

On Behalf of the Regents of the University of Michigan

By: _____ Date: _____

[NAME]

[POSITION]

Here is another example of a memorandum of understanding. It establishes the responsibilities and relationship between a public library and the library's friends group. Note in particular the legalistic vocabulary used. Note phrases like "constitute an operating agreement" and "the Friends agree to publicly support the Library and its policies," specific to this kind of document below. This memorandum of understanding could be modified to be used for an academic library friends group or for students working in a school library.

MEMORANDUM OF UNDERSTANDING BETWEEN THE FRIENDS OF THE SMITHTOWN PUBLIC LIBRARY AND THE SMITHTOWN PUBLIC LIBRARY[3]

The following will constitute an operating agreement between the Friends of the Smithtown Public Library (Friends) and the Smithtown Public Library (Library). It will stand until and unless it is modified by mutual agreement of the Board of Directors of the Friends and the Smithtown Public Library.

The Friends' mission is to raise money and public awareness in the community to support the services and programs of the Library. As a nonprofit, 501(c)3 organization, however, it is a legally distinct entity and is not a part of the Library. The Library agrees to ensure that the Friends are aware of the goals and direction of the library. The Library agrees to supply the Friends with donation requests that indicate the anticipated needs for Friends support. The Library agrees to provide the Friends with staff support to assist them with development of mailings, meeting coordination, and Friends promotional materials. The Library agrees to provide public space for Friends membership brochures and promotional materials. The Library agrees to donate used books, surplus equipment and other library property deemed to be of no immediate value to the library and not otherwise needed for library purposes to the Friends for sales whose proceeds will benefit the library. The Library agrees to provide the Friends with space in the Library for book storage and sorting for the annual book sales, and other office needs.

The Friends agree to publicly support the Library and its policies. The Friends agree to financially support the Library and its programs and services through annual donations to the library's Gift Fund and through the purchase of products and services that will benefit the library. The Friends agree to include a member from the library's administration as a nonvoting presence at all Friends' meetings and to allow room on the agenda for a library report. The Friends agree that any and all monies raised will be spent exclusively for library equipment, resources, programs, services, and other Library defined needs unless otherwise agreed to by both the Friends and the Library. The Friends agree that the library administration has the final say in accepting or declining any and all gifts made to the library. The Friends agree to engage in advocacy efforts on behalf of the Library under the guidance of the Library and the Library's Board of Trustees. The Friends agree that if they cease to actively fundraise and promote the Library, they will disband allowing for a new Friends group to be established in their stead.

A common way of making decisions at a library is by committee. For committee work not to get bogged down by disagreements or digressions, meetings are often conducted according to a set of rules. One of the more common is *Robert's Rules of Order*, which was first published in 1876. It is now in its 11th revision.

MEETING MINUTES

Meeting minutes are another variation of a memo. Minutes constitute a precis—a summary of conversations and decisions that have taken place among a committee. The format of these minutes is boilerplate: the meeting is named in the title, followed by the date and time the meeting began. Those in attendance at the meeting are named. Old business is addressed, and each of the members of the committee are asked to report out.

A SIMPLE TEMPLATE FOR MEETING MINUTES

The date and time of the meeting
List of attendees
Reading and approval of previous minutes
Old business
Reports
New business
Adjournment

BOARD OF TRUSTEES MEETING MINUTES

Call to order:
> The meeting was called to order at . . . p.m.
> Present were: . . .

Previous minutes:
> The minutes of the last meeting were read and approved.

Old business:
> There was no old business.

Reports:
> Director's report
> Secretary's report
> Treasurer's report
> Council Liaison Report:
>> Nothing new to report.
> School Liaison:
>> Nothing new to report.

New business:
The meeting was adjourned at . . .
Respectfully submitted . . .

The last kind of memo we are going to look at is an announcement of library policy. Often policies that address staff behavior are included in a HR handbook. These include the organization's dress code, response to employee tardiness, and so forth. Management often will address all staff members about the creation of a new policy or guideline instead of dealing with a problem that involves only one or two members of the library. Is there a reason this memo was sent to employees and not included in a HR handbook?

"*Parva sed potens*" is the Latin motto for the brief but mighty memo. Like the e-mail, which is often conflated with them, memos are legal forms of business correspondence. They are sometimes delivered via e-mail, which has the advantage of an automatic date stamp and clear from, to, and subject lines. The content of memos is often prescribed through office document style guides or institutional culture. When not sent through e-mail or when sent as attachments, memos have a set format in most offices, which includes using formal letterhead. When first working in a new environment, it is always good to check for model memo documents. Some offices will even specify the typeface font to use in memos.

One of the benefits of memos is that they can be used to change procedures and policies in one quick communication. Some examples of the mightiness of the memo are memos to personnel files to commemorate laudable accomplishments or to describe an event that may require disciplinary action. These are confidential memos as opposed to the public announcement form of memo to welcome a new employee, for example. Always consider your audience and the intended next steps for the memo. (Is it posted on a bulletin boards and thrown out or filed for further reference or require more action?)

As with e-mail, the subject line is the most essential content element of the memo, so make sure that the subject describes in a few words the intent of the message. In the body of the memo, be clear from the start as to the major elements of the communication. If the memo is longer than one paragraph, it may help the reader for you to categorize with headers for different parts of the memo, but always create a logical sequence and end with an invitation for comment or a simple message of thanks.

A common mistake of beginner memo writers is to make the message so short that it is incomprehensible, for example, by using incomplete sentences or acronyms with no explanations of what the letters stand for at the start. Another mistake is to send a memo in an inappropriate situation. For example, memos are not the correct form for a condolence message.

A special form of memo, the memorandum of understanding, is a procedural document that is especially useful to archives staff to make clear the responsibilities and level of care for a donated collection or item. It is always accompanied by a Deed of Gift, which is the legal document of conferral of property to be completed by the donor and the library accepting the gift. The format of memorandum of understanding is best determined by your library's legal counsel. Unlike office memos, the memorandum of understanding is not a document that you write, but more of a form to fill out. For more information on both of these forms, please consult the Society of American Archivists guides at https://www2.archivists.org/publications/brochures/deeds-of-gift.

Remember: the pen is mightier than the sword, and a well-crafted memo is the pen wielded with its sharpest point.

Mary Mallery,
Chief Librarian and Executive Director of Academic Librarians,
Brooklyn College Library

GUIDELINES FOR BRINGING CHILDREN TO WORK

Mary Frances Burns

A staff member's primary duty while at work is to perform their job duties and to serve the public. However, on occasion, it may be necessary to bring a child to work. Situations vary. Sometimes this is for a short time while waiting for a ride, for school, or for a program to start. Other times, it is for a shift. Before bringing a child to work, some questions need to be considered:

- Can your child sit quietly by his/her self and read or do homework?
- As a parent, are you comfortable letting your child sit in the Children's Room without you?
- Will the presence of the child make it uncomfortable for others to do their work?
- Is this an emergency situation caused by an overlap in schedule or a caregiver canceling?

The library appreciates that staff members are showing a sense of responsibility and demonstrating care about their jobs when bringing a child to work, rather than calling off. However, having a child at work regularly cannot substitute for child care.

Use good judgment when determining whether your child is mature enough and ready to occupy himself or herself during your work time.

Regular library policies regarding behavior apply to children at work, and it is up to the parent to enforce them (as with any situation, staff would put responsibility on the parent for the child's behavior in the library). Abiding with the library policy works both ways: if a child is at least eight years old and can sit by his or her self quietly in the Children's Room, by policy, they are welcome in the library. However, children cannot interfere while a staff member parent is "on the clock." Whether there is interference is determined by your supervisor, the person in charge, or staff in the reading room where the child is studying.

Mary Frances Burns
Director (Retired), Morley Public Library
Perry, Ohio

This memo reads very differently from the earlier memos we looked at. The verbs almost always are in the subjunctive mood, which means they express the administrator's wish for something to happen, as opposed to signifying a direct order given to staff. What would be the result if you substituted the word "must" for "should" in this section of the memo? How does it read if you eliminate some of the niceties of this request?

CHAPTER TAKEAWAY

This chapter addressed memo and memo-like documents. Memos are the most frequent kind of documentation in our profession. They are often used to issue policy or a directive. No matter what the topic, creating a template for a memo is not hard to do. What is much more difficult is finding the right tone to use to bring your audience around to your point of view.

NOTES

1. Text is adapted from Web.ics.purdue.edu/~jbay/419/memotemplate .doc.

2. An excerpt from a memo from the Office of the Vice Chancellor for Human Resources Management to College HR Directors on August 28, 2015, describing the revised Retiree E-mail Guidelines. Available at http://www.lehman.cuny.edu/itr/documents/082815_Memo_RetireeEmail Guidelines-Excerpt.pdf.

3. Reprinted with permission. All identifying materials have been removed.

SEVEN

Multifaceted Writing Projects

Some documents, like meeting minutes and agendas, are written quickly, with little thought given to language and style. However, there are other documents that require planning and coordination. These are personal, departmental, annual library reports and strategic planning documents, request for proposal (RFP), and all kinds of in-house documentation and training manuals. Like the memo, the report originally was a judicial document. *The Oxford English Dictionary* describes it as a "written account of a case heard in a court (esp. as prepared for publication), typically giving an outline of proceedings and setting out (now often verbatim) the judgment."

Unlike memos, reports aren't proscriptive. And unlike memos, clarity and careful research are valued. Reports are generally written to satisfy a need for information that has arisen in an institution.

- A description of the question
- An exploration of the question
- A review of possible solutions
- Final recommendations.

Because reports are so various in nature, it is impossible to create a one-size-fits-all template; however, a typical report is made up of these parts:

> Introduction
> Explanatory text (paragraphs 1, 2, 3 . . .)
> Conclusion/summary

Let's start by looking at one of the most common uses of a report—the establishment of a written record of what happened in the library over the course of a year. Libraries are by nature bureaucracies—some have referred to them as sophisticated ecosystems—and reports are a way of getting a handle on the overall strengths and weaknesses of the institution and the mechanics for improving them. There are many reasons a library might want to create such a report, but the major one is to justify its spending. Libraries don't generate revenue, and therefore they are under pressure to account for how they spent their budgets. Luckily, because so many library services are online, it is fairly easy to quantify their usage, using data generated in-house or by vendors. The generation of statistics is an important part of many library jobs, and it is useful for all librarians to be familiar with programs like Excel, Microsoft Access, or SPSS. If you are a graduate student and your LIS program offer courses on these tools, it is in your interest to take them. Likewise there are nonprofit organizations, like Lyrasis, that provide training in data management for working librarians.

Reports can be done at the individual, departmental, or institutional level. Depending on your work environment, you may be asked to report on your activities on a regular basis. This might be weekly, monthly, or quarterly. Most institutions ask their librarians to prepare an annual report, which is often accompanied by an annual review. An annual report is a summation of what you accomplished during the year; an annual review is an evaluation of your job performance.

Here's an example of a report a recently hired public librarian, who is in charge of the Young Adult Services, prepared for her weekly meeting with the library staff and administration.

A PERSONAL REPORT (A SMALL REPORT THAT REQUIRES DOCUMENTATION BUT LITTLE PLANNING)

My first progress report! I've only been here a month, but I have already gotten to know the staff and a few of the children and caregivers who come every morning. So far, I've been asked to look at the space through fresh eyes and see what I might recommend.

Book inventory

One of the first things I did was an inventory of the collection. We closed the children's room down for a few hours last week, and my volunteer Lucy printed out all the titles and barcodes of our books. Then the fun came trying to match them up with the books on the shelves. Andy, our part-time cataloger, will come next Thursday to re-enter any books not in the system. Started to evaluate our collection. There is a moderately good budget. Have to look at last year's circulation statistics. Put aside books that obviously need repairs.

Musical events

My predecessor set up several musical afternoons throughout the summer. She didn't keep very good records though. Note to self: need to follow up and make sure everything is in place. At my last job, we had a reading club that did very well. Would that work here? What kind of programming does well here? Have to talk to the reference librarian and see if I can find any figures.

Caldecott Winners List

Always fun to go through the latest Caldecott Winners List. Some really great titles this year. A patron dropped by a bag of books for the book sale, and I went through them. Some real classics that we can use to replace some of the worn-out books in our collection.

New rugs for the children's room

Talked to the director about sprucing up the children's room a bit. Perhaps a mural painted by one of the high school clubs? A new rug(s) donated by one of the stores in town? The director told me to make a list of what I had in mind and we will try to price out.

Staff Development
Attended PLA Webinar on collection development.
Registered for NJLA.
Mandatory staff meetings.

A school librarian might prepare a monthly report for the principal and the district's school library director that looks like this.

LINCOLN MIDDLE/JUNIOR HIGH SCHOOL

Focus for the month has been on expanding our makerspace area to make room for the 3d copy machine (purchased by the P.T.A.). After consulting with teachers, students, and our advisory committee, we've moved our makerspace area into our former microcomputer classroom from the former magazine storage area. Both areas were chosen to make it a free space for students to work without distracting students conducting research or studying in other parts of the library, but we needed more space.

Major projects included:

High school guidance counselors with students from different programs to discuss course possibilities and selection of classes for 8th grade students as they move to the high school

Accompanied 7th grade students to the all-city choir rehearsal and performance

Conducted training for teachers and student assistants on 3d copy machine

Statistics

   Book and other materials circulated:

   Number of classes conducting research in the library:

   Number of classrooms visited for specific units of instruction:

   Collaboration with teachers for future projects:

Challenges

   Synergies

   Need to get more parents and members of the community to share their expertise in our makerspace program.

It's been a busy month with the excitement of the arrival of the 3d copier. Teachers have been discussing just how to integrate this new hands-on opportunity with the wide variety of potential projects into the existing curriculum.

Below is a report prepared by a Special Collections staff member at a university. A library's mission and goals are tied in to the mission and goals of the larger institution, whether it be a school or a public or academic library. This is an example of a report organized according to the library's yearly objectives and the university's master plan.

AN ANNUAL PERSONAL REPORT THAT IS TIED INTO THE LIBRARY'S STRATEGIC PLAN

Annual report prepared by Archives and Records Services Technician

Met Objective 5:

Managed services more effectively with deeper data, randomly collected, triage of research consultations, assessment of services and teaching.

Compiled monthly statistics on research requests, reading room use, and materials tracking. Set up forms and tested two new systems for collection research request data: LibWizard and RefAnalytics. New research request tracking form will be implemented at the beginning of FY2017.

Created new call slips, to use when pulling material from the vault, and a new data entry form for potential funding of rare book conservation.

Assisted with the transition of the database from Archivists Toolkit to Archives Space.

Assisted with set up and implementation of new technologies such as Omeka and Preservica.

Review records management policies and procedures. Begin process of shifting our approach to records management to an advisory service.

Meet Objective 21:

Continued enhancing the Web site through user and Library faculty feedback

Created electronic submission forms for genealogy and sacramental requests. Rewrote Web site text to include electronic form and online payment information. Wrote blog posts to highlight new materials and interesting items in our collections.

Met Objective 22:

Digitized selected Special Collections assets to highlight the university, mission, and depth of resources.

Assisted with training of student workers on scanning photographs.

Photographed oversized materials, plaques, and ephemera. Created a file naming system for the images and input metadata into spreadsheets. Other: Researched values of our most significant rare books, and used random sampling to arrive at an estimated value for the rare book collection as a whole. . . . Coordinated details of conservation treatment of two of our rarest materials. Took over records management duties and assisted with requests and transfer of materials.

Researched records management at our peer and aspirational institutions and compiled a binder of other institutions policies and procedures for comparison. Began working with an intern to assist with the cataloging and preservation of the rare manuscript collection.

Personal Goals for FY2017

Assist with uploading authors' papers to the e-repository and with the upcoming digital humanities crowdsourcing project.

In spite of the difference in style and organizational structure, all three personal reports do exactly the same thing—they provide concrete evidence (down to the minutest of details) of the work each librarian is doing.

A last example of a departmental report is provided below.

AN ANNUAL CIRCULATION DEPARTMENT REPORT (A MEDIUM-SIZED REPORT THAT REQUIRES DEPARTMENTAL COORDINATION AND THE GENERATION OF STATISTICS)

Personnel

A circulation supervisor (Administrator) and two full-time circulation specialists (Union) and between three to five work-study students.

Departmental responsibilities: Lending services to University Library patrons. First contact with students. Maintaining the print and electronic course reserve systems. Opening and closing the library. Generating statistics and making necessary changes to ILS matrix. Supervising the use of group study rooms. First contact with campus security.

Staffing

We are now down one part-time circulation specialist—this Grade 8 position has been posted internally. The head of collection services and the circulation supervisor are collaborating to cross-train their work-study students to work in both departments.

Circulation statistics

Although our circulation statistics have decreased slightly, down to 25,000 items borrowed, the use of group study rooms and the use of the information commons has increased dramatically—this year's gate count increased to 750,000 visitors—an increase of 40 percent from last year (see the attached report for further details).

Shifting project

The circulation department was also involved in a shift of books on the third floor over the summer. Stack management handled nearly 60,000 titles.

Although these reports all have different agendas—personal (individual), personal (tied to the library's objectives), and departmental—they do share some things in common. First, they all are organized as a narrative, which means they are structured in a linear fashion with a beginning, middle, and end. Second, they are built on careful documentation.

LENGTHY REPORTS

Not every report can be completed by starting with a template. These are multifaceted projects like an accreditation report, a white paper, or a five-year plan, all of which may require contributions from an entire team. The documents are similar to earlier examples we've looked at in that their structure is formulaic. What makes them different is the amount of collaborative work that goes into producing them. The assignment may be so large that several teams of people are responsible for collecting and evaluating information. This kind of project requires careful planning and project management skills. Of course, some of these you can learn through trial and error. However, these skills also can be picked up at a library workshop or by reading one of the many books or professional articles on the subject. Luckily, these kinds of writing assignments are often the most interesting and the ones from which you can learn the most.

STRATEGIC PLANNING

Of the five rules of professional writing, the one we've discussed the least is strategy. Strategic planning is all about the end product. Just as its name implies, strategic planning is about devising a comprehensive strategy that will enable you to get from point A to point B. The word "strategy" comes from the Greek word *stratagem*, or military plan. That's exactly what you are doing when you begin an institution-wide writing project—launching a campaign. No matter how many wonderful ideas you have, your project will fail unless you have a strategy for implementing it. Large writing projects may change many times before they are finished, so you'll need to frequently refer back to your strategic plan to see if it needs to be updated as well. Be flexible.

A LIBRARY'S MASTER PLAN

In the case of a library's master plan, the objectives and goals are often determined by a library board or an institution's accrediting body. Typically, the library's new master plan is tied to changes being made on a higher institutional level. Preparing this kind of complex documentation requires that someone in authority—most likely an administrator—oversees the project. Before the administrator begins, the project manager will receive a charge from his or her superiors. Her next step is to decide on her team. Team members generally are selected because of their job responsibilities. The project manager will establish the criteria and methods that will be used to gather information for the report. The team will then work on establishing a timeline for deliverables and milestones. These might include the following objectives: interviewing faculty, staff, and students about their perceptions about the library's services; doing a comparative analysis of three of the library's peer institutions and an aspirant institution; and comparing the library's instructional plan with national and state documents.

As part of the strategic planning process, the committee makes sure the library's mission and vision statements are up-to-date. It assesses the library's current state of affairs using a standard tool like a SWOT analysis (an acronym commonly used in the corporate world that stands for strengths, weaknesses, opportunities, and threats) or a PEST analysis (an acronym which refers to the environment outside the organization, political, economic, social, and technological). When the data has been collected, generally one person writes the first draft, which is then commented on by the team. It is then presented to the library administration for review.

Creating a master plan may take a year or more. There are many strategic planning documents and library master plans on the Web. I've taken the Seattle Public Library's working draft of its master plan for 2011–2013 which is available online[1] modified it, and created a template, which you could use as a model for your own planning document.

MASTER PLAN TEMPLATE

Introduction
1. Purpose of the strategic plan
2. Major themes of the plan

Guiding Statements
Our mission . . . our vision
1. Support intellectual freedom
2. Promote literacy and a love of reading
3. Protect confidentiality of patron records
4. Foster a healthy democracy
5. Form strong partnerships
6. Advance and innovate

Summary of Goals and Objectives
1. Fuel your community's passion for reading, personal growth and learning
2. Expand your community's access to information, ideas, and stories
3. Empower your community's distinctive communities & vibrant neighborhoods
4. Build partnerships to make a difference in people's lives
5. Foster an organizational culture of innovation

Appendices

ANNUAL REPORT

Other than a multiyear strategic plan, an annual report is one of the most time-consuming documents to prepare. Like other lengthy reports, it involves collecting and analyzing statistics, preparing and presenting data, and creating a persuasive narrative to hold it all together. Luckily, an annual report is a highly formulaic document that's easy to reproduce. An annual report template might look like this:

TEMPLATE FOR AN ANNUAL REPORT

Mission statement
Library objectives
Major accomplishments
Departmental objectives
Personnel reports (appointments, promotions, professional activities)
Budget
Major gifts and contributions

Let's take the example of preparing an annual report for a small community college library. After discussions with the library director and the staff, the team project manager decides five kinds of data are needed: interlibrary loan statistics, circulation statistics, collection development statistics, budget allocation and expenditures, and individual staff reports.

The first step is to make a table that contains each of the data points.

LIBRARY ANNUAL REPORT

Interlibrary Loan Statistics

Circulation Statistics

Collection Development Statistics

Budget Allocation and Expenditures

Staff Development (Individual Reports)

Once our categories are established, we can look at each of the sections and decide who will be responsible for providing information—in the case of interlibrary loan, access services, collection development, and staff development, for example, the most likely person would be the departmental head.

Since data drives most of the decisions made in libraries, we'll revise the chart, so it looks something like this:

Tasks	Person	Format	Department
Lending and borrowing statistics	Martha	Excel	Interlibrary loan
Circulation statistics, lost books, shelving	Julia	Excel	Circulation
eBook, print books, e-journal statistics	James	Excel	Collection development
Staff attendance at conferences, training sessions, seminars	Peter	Word	Administration

The next set of tasks constitutes establishing the timeline.

Categories	When is the data going to be collected	When is the statistical analysis for each report going to be finished	When is the due date to submit this section of the report to the project leader
Interlibrary loan	6/1	8/1	9/1
Collection development	5/15	7/15	8/1
Circulation	4/4	6/4	7/1
Administration	6/3	(no statistical analysis; information gathered from individual reports)	9/2

The final data, which can now be incorporated into the report, would look like this:

Circulation (monographs circulated, article downloads, e-repository downloads)

Monographs circulated: 2,000; Article downloads: 600,000; E-repository downloads: 400,000.

Collection Development (general collection, items added, items withdrawn)

Total volumes: 4 million; Items added this year: 2,000; Journals: 300; Special Collections: 3,500 linear feet; Items digitized: 30,000.

Staff Development:

23 in-house presentations attended, 12 state workshops, 8 conference presentations.

Now it would be up to the project manager to work with his or her team to pull the entire document together.

Once you understand how the templates are structured, you will be able to complete your own report without difficulty, provided you have access to the data you need.

Let's look at another example of a school library annual report.

The Johnson City Elementary School Library serves 800 students, grades K–5 (24 classrooms plus art, vocal and instrumental music, a nurse, physical education, a guidance counselor, and two library staff) on the edge of suburbia with some students being bused to the school. One-third of these children come from single parent homes while others live in homes surrounding the country club golf course. The purpose of the library is to provide a level playing field for all the students.

Our goals include the following:

- Bring the Johnson City Elementary School Library staff, program, and collection to meet the teaching and learning needs of all the students and teachers
- Ensure that all students have access and learning to use the equipment needed to survive in a technological world. To provide an environment where all students achieve to the best of their ability

Highlights of the year

We have achieved phase three of our five-year plan and have added a full-time library technician to our staff. This has allowed us to strengthen our technology component by installing a wireless network throughout the school, providing notebook computers for each student, and allowing teachers to create more online resources for students. We have increased our relationship with the public library so that students may use their Internet facilities after school hours. We have also increased our training sessions for parents, so they are better prepared to help their children with this increase in technology and use of online course materials.

Our technician has trained 100 of our fourth and fifth grade students to serve as technology assistants in their classes. They are able to help new students to our school master their computers and to assist teachers when they need to learn a new application. We see this introduction to the world of technology as one of our efforts to demonstrate a life after high school and encourage all the students to plan to stay in school through middle and high school.

This technician has also been able to train many parents, including those who volunteer to work in our library, as well as others, so that they are aware of the challenges facing their children.

The purchase of new moveable furniture and shelving has allowed us to reconfigure the library throughout the day, encouraging heavier use of the library for collaborative units of instruction and making the library readily available for different grouping of students for a wider variety of activities.

Trends

New state guidelines are being developed for teaching science, math, and history. It is anticipated that implementation of these guidelines will affect the programming in the library, and we are preparing for this.

Significant projects

We are joining the coalition of schools, the public library, the local community college, and the Johnson City Chamber of Commerce for "Project Future," an effort to show students, beginning in kindergarten through high school, the benefits of remaining in school in terms of life after high school. We are hoping that by beginning in elementary, we can reduce the dropout rate of our students.

Statistics totals

With the increase in staffing, our statistics show a growth from the previous year to the present in all areas.

Activity	Last Year	This Year	Comments below reflect the consensus of the library staff
Class visits the library	600	680	
Collaborative units with teachers	6	18	
# parent volunteers	15	19	
# parents/community members working with makerspaces	5	15	
# outside speakers	3	15	
# technology sessions with teachers	5	15	
# technology sessions with parents	0	10	This does not include open house night with parents dropping by
Total resources added			Of these, 100 were
Books	300	400	e-books
Databases	2	8	Notebooks make these essential
Total equipment added Notebook computers	10	1,000	

Planning for the future

Training teachers and students on how to make the best use of our present technologies is ongoing. However, in the future, these technologies will change, and new software will provide new challenges. An additional staff member will be needed.

Purchasing new equipment that is easily moved to accommodate individuals and small groups working on projects means heavier use of the library. This and the potential changes in technologies make hiring another staff member essential.

Budget for the purchase of computer software for upgrading systems is presently provided from the district technology office, and this has allowed us to add databases to our collection.

Here is the same report reduced to its most basic elements—our template.

ELEMENTARY SCHOOL LIBRARY ANNUAL REPORT
Table of Contents
Highlights
Trends in Curriculum
Student Learning Objectives
Professional Activities
Volunteers
Donations
Circulation
Collection
Technology
Databases

Lastly, here is a university library's annual report that has been reduced to its most basic elements.

UNIVERSITY LIBRARY ANNUAL REPORT
Message from the dean of the library
2015 Highlights
Strategic directions
Staff recognition and service
Honor role of donors
Inputs and outputs

DATA-DRIVEN DECISION MAKING

Library administrators rely on data to drive their decision making. Unlike educators, who may have to wait years to see whether their teaching has had any impact on their students, librarians have immediate access to in-house data, like circulation and interlibrary loan statistics, and vendor data, like article downloads, to guide their planning That data is usually of two kinds: qualitative and quantitative. Qualitative data is data that is descriptive, such as the results of a survey on user satisfaction. Quantitative data is data that can be measured, such as the annual number of books a library circulates. Both kinds of data require some kind of human mediation in order to be interpreted and both are used in preparing an annual report. Some libraries use inputs and outputs as measurements as well. Inputs are quantitative measurements of the items a library spends money on (like databases and monographs). Outputs are quantitative measurements of a library's activities (like programming).

RFPs

Publicly financed university and college libraries, state libraries, and local libraries are required by law to solicit competing bids from vendors for large-scale projects they plan to undertake. These kinds of projects often are funded through bond offerings or another kind of debt that has to be approved through a public referendum. Before issuing a request for proposal (RFP), a library may also ask for information (RFI) from vendors about their qualifications. Sometimes a request for quotation (RFQ) is sent to individual vendors to get a clarification of the terms of their bid. An RFP is not a report—it's a bid—but the structure is similar.

Private institutions, like universities, also use RFPs to solicit bids for big-ticket items like a library expansion or the purchase of a new library ILS (integrated library system), since these projects must be budgeted for at the institutional level. At a minimum, an RFP consists of the project description, its timeline, and the functional specifications vendors will be bidding on. A larger project may include a description of the organization, the scope of the project, its functional requirements, target audience, budget, proposal guidelines and vendor qualifications.

A BRIEF RFP

A good example of a brief RFP can be found in ALA's RFP to solicit vendor bids for its new Website, "RFP for a SaaS Community Platform."[2] Here is a brief example for a project with technical specifications.

A TECHNOLOGY PROPOSAL

Institutional Overview

1. Project Overview

   a. Project scope
   b. Timeline

2. Proposal Content

   a. Company Information
   b. Cost
   c. Response to Functional Requirement Specifications
   d. Implementation Plan
   e. Training Plan
   f. Warranty Maintenance and Support

3. RFP Terms and Conditions

4. Functional Requirement Specifications

   a. General System Requirement Specification
   You can specify the general system requirements from the following aspects: reliability, architecture, data security, authentication and identity management, interoperability and extensibility, migration, and vendor support.
   b. Technical Services
   Organize the specifications by functionalities
   c. Public Services

5. Contract to be signed by end of June

6. Work to begin mid-July

7. Launch date in late September

Like the first example, this one can be divided into three parts: an overview of the organization, a description of the project, and a timeline.

**PROPOSAL AND DOCUMENTATION FOR A LARGE
LIBRARY BUILDING PROJECT[3]**

Table of Contents
   I. Purpose
   II. Background and Introductory Statement
   III. Overview
   IV. Project Description
   V. Scope of Work
   VI. Submission Requirements
   VII. Additional Information

VIII. Required Forms for Submission
- Americans with Disabilities Act of 1990
- Township of Maplewood Noncollusion Affidavit
- Mandatory Equal Opportunity and Affirmative Action Language
- Statement of Ownership/Stockholder Disclosure Certification
- Pay to Play—Business Entity Disclosure Certification (accompanying this RFP as a Word document)

IX. Library Building Program (accompanying this RFP as a PDF document)

The opposite of creating an RFP is to request funding from your own funding source or from an outside agency. The information you will need to include is the same for all, and the only difference is the amount of information to be included.

A SIMPLE REQUEST FOR FUNDING TEMPLATE

Project Title
Goal
Objectives
Activities
Evaluation
Dissemination
Staff
Budget

When this information is directed at the library's main funding source, it may be seen as justification for an item not in the budget. For a school, this might be the purchase of a 3d copy machine for the Makerspace area, and it is simply a description of what is needed and why.

[Title] 3d Copier
[Goal] Students in our school need to turn their creative ideas into three-dimensional objects.
[Objective] It is estimated that every student will be able to create at least one object this school year.
[Activities] The 3d copier will be available in the Makerspace area where teachers and volunteers from the community will help the students create products after a creative design process.
[Evaluation] Each project will be on display in the library showcase for at least two weeks throughout the year as they are created.

[Dissemination] Parents and caregivers will be invited to the school when their child's object is on display. Also, an evening event will be held near the end of the school year in the cafeteria for student-selected projects. The superintendent, central office staff, school board and community will be invited to honor students, [staff] teachers, and the community volunteers who have been assisting in this project.

[Budget] Attached you will find a request for a bid for a 3d copier. It is anticipated that the range for this purchase will be from $– to $–.

An academic or public library might be more likely to request funding from a local foundation or another in the *Foundation Directory*. This will be a simple letter detailing the request.

School librarians have had success applying for the Laura Bush Foundation for America's Libraries. This foundation "provides funds to our nation's neediest schools so they can extend, update, and diversify the book and print collections in their schools with the goal of encouraging students to develop a love of reading and learning." Information about these grants can be found at www.laurabushfoundation.com.

IN-HOUSE INSTRUCTIONAL MANUALS

Our last example is an in-house instructional manual. Most often, these involve the processing of library materials, but in-house manuals can have other purposes as well. Students and nonlibrarian staff frequently receive training to introduce them to functions like circulation and interlibrary loan and to provide guidance on how to interact with the public. Because procedures change, in-house manuals are frequently updated. Below is the table of contents of a processing manual produced for small archival repositories in Alaska.[4]

ARCHIVAL PROCESSING MANUAL

Section 1: Introduction

1.1: Core Concepts
1.2: Types of Collections
1.3: Finding Aids

Section 2: Appraisal, Duplicates, Discards, and Scheduled Records

2.1: Value of Materials
2.2: Publications
2.3: Duplicates

2.4: Discards
2.5: Scheduled Records

Section 3: Processing

3.1: Preliminary Research
3.2: Creating and Ordering Series
3.3: Creating a Processing Plan
3.4: Sorting the Collection
3.5: Putting Materials into Folders
3.6: Putting Folders into Boxes
3.7: Labeling Folders
3.8: Oversized Items
3.9: Labeling Boxes

Section 4: Creating the Finding Aid

4.1: Overview
4.2: Create a New Resource Record
4.3: Writing the Front Matter
4.4: Entering the Container List
4.5: Formatting Concerns
4.6: Finishing Up

Appendices

Appendix A: Unit History
Appendix B: Well-Written Finding Aid Components

Thus far, we have focused our attention on taking simple and complex examples of the three kinds of documents most often used by librarians in their daily work—the memo, the report, and the letter—and repurposing them for our own uses. We've called this the "template method" and this process "templating." This last transformative example is the most challenging so far because it shows how to take a document that is only tangentially related to yours and creatively alter it to become something quite different.

USING AN ARCHIVAL PROCESSING MANUAL AS THE BASIS OF A COLLECTION SERVICES DEPARTMENT REPORT

Although the table of contents we just looked at is for an archival processing manual, it easily could be repurposed to serve a template for another kind of document.

Archival Processing Manual	**Collection Services policies and procedures**
Section 1: Introduction	**Section 1: Introduction**
1.1: Core Concepts	1.1: Core functions of the department
1.2: Types of Collections	
1.3: Finding Aids	1.2: Types of collections
	1.3: Staff workflow
	1.4: Staff priorities in order of importance
Section 2: Appraisal, Duplicates, Discards, and Scheduled Records	**Section 2: Collection development policies**
2.1: Value of Materials	2.1: Policies for new book acquisitions
2.2: Publications	
2.3: Duplicates	2.2: Policies for faculty requests
2.4: Discards	2.3: Policies for duplicates
2.5: Scheduled Records	2.4: Policies for discards
	2.5: Policies for gift books
Section 3: Processing	**Section 3: Acquisitions**
3.1: Preliminary Research	3.1: Procedures for purchasing print book acquisitions
3.2: Creating and Ordering Series	
3.3: Creating a Processing Plan	3.2: Procedures for purchasing e-books
3.4: Sorting the Collection	
3.5: Putting Materials into Folders	3.3; Procedures for purchasing e-journals
3.6: Putting Folders into Boxes	
3.7: Labeling Folders	3.4: Procedures for purchasing print journals
3.8: Oversized Items	
3.9: Labeling Boxes	
Section 4: Creating the Finding Aid	**Section 4: Adding materials to the knowledge base and the catalog**
4.1. Overview	
4.2: Create a New Resource Record	4.1: Create a new resource record in the catalog

(continued)

(continued)

Archival Processing Manual	Collection Services policies and procedures
4.3: Writing the Front Matter	4.2: Enter data in the knowledge base
4.4: Entering the Container List	
4.5: Formatting Concerns	4.3: Checking the catalog display
4.6: Finishing Up	

CHAPTER TAKEAWAY

Reports are the most time-consuming and difficult documents to write. They are often requested when a library administration needs data in order to make a decision. Types of reports include strategic planning documents, annual reviews, and so forth. There are some documents, like RFPs, whose format is determined by legal and other restrictions yet are more like reports than memos or letters—the two other genres of professional writing.

NOTES

1. "Strategic Plan," Seattle Public Library, http://clerk.seattle.gov/~public /meetingrecords/2011/cbriefing20110103_5b.pdf.

2. "RFP for a SaaS Community Platform," American Library Association, Accessed first through https://itts.ala.org/news/2015/05/04/ala-rfp-for -a-saas-community-platform/.

3. "Request for Proposal," Maplewood Library, July 13, 3016, http:// www.maplewoodlibrary.org/main/uploads/Request-for-Proposal.pdf.

4. "ASU Processing Manual," Archivists.org, March 2015, https:// www2.archivists.org/sites/all/files/asu_processing_manual.pdf.

EIGHT

Newsletters, News Stories, Press Releases, Library Correspondence, and Surveys

Newsletters, news stories, press releases, are all documents that provide current and factual information. News stories tend to share the same organizational structure, called an inverted pyramid. This means that the most important information is placed at the beginning of the document, and the least important is at the end.

THE INVERTED PYRAMID

The lead sentence
Second most important piece of information
Third most important piece of information

NEWSLETTER

The newsletter is a medium in transition; we could have just as well placed it in the chapter on digital formats. Although print newsletters still exist, most library newsletters now are created online. Social media allows libraries to take advantage of marketing tools that don't exist in a two-dimensional environment like print. Hybrid forms of newsletters can be found on Facebook or in a library blog and can be accessed through

Twitter or Instagram. What is the difference between a newsletter and a blog? Newsletters generally have a fixed layout and are published on a regular basis. Blogs entries are published at the discretion of the writer and reflect topics of current interest to the author.

In putting together a library newsletter, you will want to consider what news is important to your patrons. Are you planning a lecture for seniors on Social Security and Medicare benefits? Which novel will the book club be reading next? When is the next library board meeting? All these are appropriate topics for a newsletter. You can download newsletter templates on the Web, for free or for a small cost. Alternately, if you have a blogging program like WordPress you can add a newsletter extension plug in and easily create one.

A SIMPLE NEWSLETTER TEMPLATE

Welcome
Upcoming general programs and events
Upcoming teen programs and events
Upcoming children's programs and events
Library calendar
Report on new acquisitions and services

Newsletter entries often include a calendar of events. For a book sale announcement (below) you would include the date of the sale, the last date materials will be accepted, and what kind of materials should be donated.

FRIENDS OF THE LIBRARY NEWS

The Friends of the Library will be accepting gently used books, CDs, and DVDs for the Annual Book Sale. Bring your donations to the rear entrance of the library and deposit them in the hallway. Please donate books that are in good condition. We do not accept textbooks or encyclopedias. The book sale begins on March 11.

NEWS STORIES

Local news stories by or about the library generally focus on events like speaker series, a library expansion, and the approval or rejection of a library budget. Sometimes a news story will be of interest to a larger readership. This is what happened, for example, with the proposed controversial renovation of New York City Public Library's 40th Street branch, which was covered for several months by the *New York Times*. But whatever the publication, the organizational structure of a news piece is the same. The lead paragraph provides a summary of the news piece. If the reader only has a short amount of time, he or she can read the first paragraph and skim the rest of the article. If the story runs over the word limit, the newspaper editor will cut from the bottom.

TEMPLATE OF A NEWS STORY

Headline
Byline
Lead paragraph
Less important paragraph
Even less important paragraph

NEWS BRIEF

The news piece below reports an ALA relief effort.[1] Notice how focused the headline is. What is the most important theme or topic being discussed?

School Raises Money to Support Haiti's Libraries: Kansas Elementary Students' "Bucks for Books" Benefits ALA Relief Efforts

Throughout February, students at Wanamaker Elementary School in Topeka, Kansas, brought pennies, nickels, dimes, quarters, and dollars to class for the school's annual Bucks for Books fundraiser, now in its fifth year. "We tie some education with it," says Alice Reinert, school librarian at Wanamaker. "It's geared to help our younger students learn their coins. And it's also to try to get them service minded." February is also when Wanamaker holds its Book Fair, so the month was a celebration of books and literacy, Reinert says. At the end of the three-week fundraiser, students raised a little more than $1,600, and they decided to donate $2,000 to the American Library Association's (ALA) Haiti Library Relief Fund. That money includes $1,000 from this year's fundraiser and $1,000 from last year's, which hadn't yet been disbursed. The remaining $600 was divided between the library at Topeka Rescue Mission, a local homeless shelter, and the Wanamaker Elementary library. "[Students] liked the idea that it was going to support literacy all the way, 100 percent," Reinert says. "They wanted to not just help a local cause, and not just here in our own school, but they wanted to go far globally."

Although this article excerpt is written in a chatty, colloquial style it follows the typical structure of a news piece, starting with a lead that invites the reader to pay attention. This kind of device is called the "the hook," because the opening sentence literally "hooks" you into reading further. Can you identify what part of the sentence acts as the hook? The information in the article is front loaded, so if you lose interest you will still know what the article is about.

BELOIT DAILY NEWS BRIEF ON CHILDREN LIBRARY ACTIVITIES

I have been a Children's Librarian for almost eight years and I have a confession. Up until about six weeks ago, I had never done a story time. I had never actually sat down and read a story or sung The Itsy-Bitsy Spider or Twinkle, Twinkle, Little Star to a group of kids. Shocking, isn't it? Now mind you, it wasn't because I don't like kids. And it wasn't because I don't like books. It was because the Beloit Public Library has Youth Services staff who do story times way, way better than I could ever hope to do them. And, truth be told, I really don't like singing in front of people. Singing in the car, radio up full blast? That's a different story.

Now that I have a few story times under my belt, I'm pleasantly surprised at how much I enjoy doing them. I think I like them so much because I get to read picture books...[2]

Jeni Schomber,
Head of Youth Services,
Beloit Public Library

A PRESS RELEASE

A press release may be a news story written by a library or a library organization to promote an event. Press releases also may be written and distributed by a public relations firm. Sometimes a press release will be picked up by a newspaper and run without changes. Other times a press release will be used as the basis of a news story. Generally, a press release contains a great deal of factual information. Similar to a news story, the most important information of a press release can be found in the headline and the first paragraph. The press release below describes the creation of a new information hub in Manhattan.[3] Pay particular attention to the choice of verbs.

The New York Public Library and the McGraw-Hill Companies Open "Financial Literacy Central"

New York, June 3, 2010—The New York Public Library and The McGraw-Hill Companies (NYSE: MHP) today unveiled a new information hub in the heart of Manhattan that is dedicated to improving New Yorkers' personal finances.

Financial Literacy Central, located at 188 Madison Avenue at 34th Street in the Science, Industry and Business Library (SIBL), provides the public with free one-on-one sessions with financial planners through the Financial Planning Association; computer access to popular business and finance databases; 1,500 books on a wide range of financial topics—including more than 100 McGraw-Hill Education titles donated by The McGraw-Hill Companies—and financially focused classes.

The new center, which is expected to reach 20,000 patrons by the end of the year, will complement the City of New York's Office of Financial Empowerment by offering another educational resource to help New Yorkers make sensible money decisions. In addition, librarians at The New York Public Library's 90 neighborhood branches are being trained to help patrons find authoritative online resources about personal finance issues.

"Education is the key that unlocks economic empowerment. As we open the doors to this world class facility, we also help open the doors to a secure financial future for tens of thousands of New Yorkers," said Harold McGraw III, chairman, president and chief executive officer of The McGraw-Hill Companies. "The New York Public Library is one of the city's most vital institutions, and we are proud to expand our partnership and support of its ongoing mission of inspiring lifelong learning, advancing knowledge, and strengthening our communities."

The press release below describes a lavish new library publication. Note the contact information placed at the beginning of the document.

CARD CATALOG'S HISTORY IS FOCUS OF NEW LIBRARY PUBLICATION[4]

Press Contact: Jennifer Gavin (202) 707-1940
Public Contact: Diane Levinson, Chronicle Books, diane_levinson@chronicle-books.com
Website: Order the book from the Library Shop External

A new book exploring the history of the card catalog—that venerated chest of small drawers that contained the known universe, has been published by the Library of Congress in association with Chronicle Books. The lavishly illustrated volume tells the story of libraries' organizing approaches—from the layout of papyrus scrolls at the Library of Alexandria and playing cards with notes on the back that served librarians during the chaos of the French Revolution—to the doorstep of the digital information retrieval we use today. The card catalog evolved out of the need for a standardized system to manage rapidly expanding libraries, serving as both a repository for data and a search tool in a pre-digital age.

"The Card Catalog: Books, Cards, and Literary Treasures," includes illustrations featuring the Library's original catalog cards (many with fascinating annotations) and the covers of many familiar, beloved books in its collections. Librarian of Congress Carla Hayden contributed the foreword, declaring the card catalog "the gateway to the wonders of a library's collection" in the 20th century.

"The Card Catalog" traces the catalog from its earliest precursors through the height of its popularity and eventual transition to online methods. The Library of Congress, after decades of reliance on a system originally devised by Thomas Jefferson for his own books, created its own card cataloging system as the 20th century began and for decades made its cards available to local public libraries nationwide. "The Card Catalog" features many of these original cards, both handwritten and typed, with notations and stamps reflecting the work of generations of librarians.

Paired with the cards are photographs of some of the great treasures in the Library's collection, from Shakespeare's "First Folio" and Walt Whitman's corrections on a print of "O Captain! My Captain!" to first editions of "The Adventures of Huckleberry Finn" and "To Kill a Mockingbird."

"The Card Catalog," a 224-page hardcover book with more than 200 color illustrations, is available for $35 in the Library of Congress Shop, 10 First St. S.E., Washington, D.C., 20540-4985. Credit-card orders are taken at (888) 682-3557 or loc.gov/shop/.

The Library of Congress is the world's largest library, offering access to the creative record of the United States—and extensive materials from around the world—both on-site and online. It is the main research arm of the U.S. Congress and the home of the U.S. Copyright Office. Explore collections, reference services and other programs and plan a visit at loc.gov, access the official site for U.S. federal legislative information at congress.gov, and register creative works of authorship at copyright.gov.

This press release created by the American Library Association for National Library Week is a template in the true sense of the word, because all you have to do is fill in the blanks. This association, as many others, would like its members to support its position of a variety of issues and providing a template makes it easier for them to do so.

For release National Library Week
April 13–19, 2014
Contact: (name, title, phone number)
Lives change @ your library: celebrate National Library Week April 13–19
(CITY, STATE)—This week, the [name of library] joins libraries in schools, campuses and communities nationwide in celebrating National Library Week, a time to highlight the value of libraries, librarians and library workers.

Libraries today are more than repositories for books and other resources. Often the heart of their communities, campuses or schools, libraries are deeply committed to the places where their patrons live, work and study. Libraries are trusted places where everyone in the community can gather to reconnect and reengage with each other to enrich and shape the community and address local issues.

Librarians work with elected officials, small business owners, students and the public at large to discover what their communities' needs are and meet them. Whether through offering e-books and technology classes, materials for English-language learners, programs for job seekers or those to support early literacy, librarians listen to the community they serve, and they respond.

The [name of the library] serves [name of city/school/college] by providing [list services/resources.]

"Service to the community has always been the focus of the library," said [name and title of the spokesperson]. "While this aspect has never changed, libraries have grown and evolved in how they provide for the needs of every member of their community."

The [name of library] is celebrating National Library Week by [describe programs, activities here].

First sponsored in 1958, National Library Week is a national observance sponsored by the American Library Association (ALA) and libraries across the country each April.

For more information, visit the [name of library] at [address], call [phone number] or see the library's Web site at [provide URL]. Libraries hours are [list times].[5]

CORRESPONDENCE

For many generations, letter writing was taught as part of the grammar school curriculum, along with penmanship. But with the advent of modern communications, letter writing gradually died out, and today has been replaced by e-mail. Librarians more often communicate through memos rather than through letters, because the memo is a better vehicle for delivering administrative news. However, there are professional situations that benefit from personal correspondence. These are the times when you need to establish or reinforce a personal connection with an individual.

Generally, if you are writing a handwritten note to an employee, a board or community member, or a volunteer, you should pick good quality bond paper or use your institution's stationery and write with a black or blue pen. And it is always a good idea to sign a letter, even if it has been written on a computer.

Letter writing is a particularly difficult genre to master because it is so dependent on the nuances of language. Let's say for example that you want to write a letter to a member of the Friends of the Library, thanking her for organizing the monthly exhibits in the children's room throughout the year. To personalize your letter, you might buy a lovely card or include a frame to mount the correspondence in. You might want to start with a draft to find the right tone to express your gratitude. Of course, you'd stress the volunteer's generosity for sharing her time and expertise, and you'd comment on how well received the monthly exhibits were. Although generosity is a term that would be appropriate, you also might want to look at a thesaurus to find synonyms that might be even better: kindness, bigheartedness, openhandedness, and so forth. If you work at an academic library, read through some of the thank-you letters prepared by university advancement, and you will see that each one strikes a different tone, depending on the audience that is being addressed. The basic template of a letter is quite simple and was discussed earlier in the section on e-mail.

LETTER TEMPLATE

Date

address
Salutation
Text
Salutation
Name/signature

Let's take a look at two letters written by board members that aim to establish a personal relationship with the recipient. In the first, the author asks a patron to fulfill her promise to give a donation to the library; in the second, the author responds to a news article critical of the library's decision to undertake an expansion.

Ms. xxx
259 Anywhere Road
Anywhere, USA

Dear xxx,

Recently you pledged to help the Citizens for our Library pass the Library's Levy renewal by giving financial support to the campaign. The time has come to do so. Your donation will help us send literature to absentee voters and to purchase an endorsement ad in the newspaper in support of the campaign.

Any support that you can give is appreciated. Please make your check out to the Any Name Library. Enclosed is an addressed envelope for your convenience. If it is more convenient, please feel free to drop the envelope off at the library.

Your donation will ensure that the library will continue to offer the excellent service for which it is known.

Thank you.
Sincerely;

Joe Smith
Any Name Library

CHAPTER TAKEAWAY

We've addressed two different kinds of professional writing in this chapter. The first is news documents that is a subgenre of the report. News documents are for the most part fact based and generally employ some kind of heightened language—the hook—to draw the reader in. Personal correspondence, although infrequently used in a library setting, is still an important means of communicating in our profession. This is an old-fashioned medium, and standard conventions apply both to its language and presentation.

NOTES

1. A. Marcotte, "School Raises Money to Support Haiti's Libraries," *American Libraries*, April 13, 2017, https://americanlibrariesmagazine .org/blogs/the-scoop/school-raises-money-to-support-haitis-libraries.

2. Beloit Library, October 2016, http://www.beloitlibrary.info/sites /default/files/bdnarticles/2016/October%202016.pdf. Originally published in the *Beloit Daily News*, October 26, 2016.

3. "The New York Public Library and the McGraw-Hill Companies Open 'Financial Literacy Central,'" New York Public Library, June 2, 2010, https://www.nypl.org/press/press-release/2010/06/02/fianncial -planning-hard-times-nypl-unveil-financial-literacy-central-.

4. Available at https://loc.gov/item/prn-17-050/.

5. "National Library Week 2014—Sample Press Release," American Library Association, April 2014, http://www.ala.org/conferencesevents /national-library-week-sample-press-release.

NINE

Résumés, Job Advertisements, Cover Letters, and Job Recommendation Letters

Employment opportunities for librarians tend to follow the fortunes of the economy. Librarians who have graduated from a program accredited by the American Library Association's Committee on Accreditation often have a distinct advantage in applying for jobs at educational institutions, corporate archives, and special libraries because their terminal degree, a masters in library and information science, acts as a licensing certificate. This is less often the case with IT jobs, which require that applicants have a knowledge of or certification in programming languages.

Whatever kind of employment you aspire to, writing is central to the job search. In the process of looking for a job, you will have to put together a curriculum vita (CV), write a persuasive cover letter, and correspond with the human resources department and the search committee if there is one.

RÉSUMÉS AND CVs

What is the difference between a résumé and a CV? A résumé is a summary of your work experience. It should include your contact information, educational background, and the names of the institutions you have worked for, as well as your dates of employment and job responsibilities. A résumé is most often used in the business world.

A CV is much longer—in the case of a mid-career librarian it might be as many as 15 or 20 pages—and lists significant achievements in your working life. A CV is generally required for jobs that are academic in nature.

A template for a CV might look something like this:

CONTACT INFORMATION

Name
Address
E-mail
Cell

EDUCATION

Reverse order: current to earliest; include year of graduation, university name, dates degrees were obtained (i.e., January 2012–present).

EMPLOYMENT

Reverse order: current to earliest; include name of company/organization; brief job description, dates of employment (i.e., January 2012–present).

LANGUAGES AND PROFICIENCIES

Include if appropriate.

SPECIALIZED COURSEWORK, TRAINING, OR CERTIFICATES

AFFILIATIONS

Membership in civic, library, and other associations. Date range; position held.

Whether you have just been hired, are looking for a job, or have held your position for a long time, you should be keeping your résumé or CV up-to-date. The easiest way to do this is to create a master document that you can add to. You might do this when your job responsibilities increase, you receive an award or commendation, or you have authored a publication or given a presentation. A CV is actually quite difficult to write because there is no single template. In fact, a CV or résumé should be revised every time you go on a job interview in order to make sure you tailor your skills and experiences to the needs of the employer. These same skills and experiences also should be emphasized in the cover letter that you send to the search committee. For example, if you were applying for a job as an instructional librarian, you would highlight your teaching experience and knowledge of state and national information literacy standards. You also might stress your facility with common library e-tools, like LibGuides or citation management systems. If, on the other hand, you were applying for a job as a business librarian, you might mention your teaching experience, but you would draw attention to your degree in economics and training on business databases.

Tips on Résumés, Cover Letters, and References

Over the years and decades of a career, one picks up tips from mentors, and through service on search committees. Here are a few to consider.

Length of cover letter. Early career the letter should not exceed two pages, single spaced. Mid to later in career, it should not exceed three pages. The truth is, many employers look at the résumé first to screen for required skills and experience. The cover letter is often a yardstick to gauge communication and writing skills and important accomplishments. Just don't spill out your entire career in the letter. Keep it concise, positive, and accurate. Catch the reader's interest.

A quick way to the rejection basket. Spelling, punctuation, and grammar must be perfect with all submitted application materials. Misspellings are an immediate turnoff and indicate lack of attention to detail and professionalism. Have a colleague proofread all materials, including cover letter, résumé/CV, and lists of references. Don't rely on spell-check.

References. Try to include at least one more reference than is requested, preferably two. If they ask for three, submit four or five. Reason: Employer may be unable to reach one or two references. Also, this practice just looks good. It communicates that the applicant is well-known and has professional connections.

More on references. It may seem obvious, but select references who you know will speak positively. This may not always be possible with supervisors, and if there is an issue with the current supervisor, try to include a former supervisor. Also, as a courtesy, describe in the reference roster the relationship in which you know the reference.

Show results! The letter should be written in active tense and show results: Use words and phrases like: "chaired special project on," "led effort to," "resulting in," "reengineered," "secured grant on," and "reorganized."

Qualifications. Speak to every required, and if possible preferred, qualification in the cover letter. Search committees look for ways to reject applicants and will often use checklists. Make it easy for them to forward you to the next round of consideration. Don't make them hunt in your résumé/CV for your experience on X, Y, and Z.

Sometimes less is better. Be careful about listing personal interests, memberships, family information in application materials, unless they add direct value to the job. If some are included, keep the list tilted toward community service. The employer is hiring you for your professional abilities. Personal interests and background are fine to share at appropriate times during the on-site interview.

You've done your research. Mention something about the institution or library early in the letter, and how it relates to your accomplishments. Example: "Your library's campus leadership on textbook affordability is impressive. I am developing a list of OER [open educational resource] textbooks that we are sharing in outreach efforts with our teaching faculty."

Keep it simple. For all application materials, it is usually best to adopt a more restrained tone. Use standard fonts; avoid colored text and excessive stylization, such as italics, emojis, exclamation marks, and so on. Bio photographs are generally not necessary. The content should sell itself.

Frank R. Allen,
Senior Associate Director for Administrative Services,
University of Central Florida Libraries

JOB ADVERTISEMENTS

Job advertisements are generally posted on library blogs, iSchool and LIS Web sites, or mega job search sites. These advertisements follow a simple formula that looks something like this:

JOB ADVERTISEMENT TEMPLATE

Information about the organization
Job description
Required qualifications
Preferred qualifications
Legal disclaimers

Job advertisements can be vague and even contradictory about the kind of employee that the institution is looking for. Part of this is intentional because a lack of clarity allows the library to cast a wide net for applicants. But it is also true that institutions often don't know what they actually need in an employee, so they rely on pro-forma descriptions to fill a job position.

Although it seems obvious, the most important thing you can do when applying for a job is to read the job advertisement carefully. Below is an ad for a catalog management librarian.[1] Let's try to determine what kind of employee the library is looking for and how the job applicant should shape his or her response. Notice the minimum qualifications for this position, as well as the preferred qualifications.

MANAGEMENT LIBRARIAN, UNIVERSITY OF NORTH TEXAS
POSITION ANNOUNCEMENT: CATALOG LIBRARIAN

The University of North Texas seeks experienced multi-tasking, detail-oriented candidates for a Catalog Management Librarian position. Cataloging librarians improve the research experiences of, and save the time of, our users by providing a thoroughly functional search interface enhanced with standardized subject headings, updated authority records, and accurate bibliographic information.

Reporting to the Head of Cataloging and Metadata Services (CMS), *this librarian is responsible for catalog records and related data for monographs and continuing resources in a variety of formats.* The librarian will work collaboratively within the CMS department to maintain a comprehensive and precise catalog of holdings for the UNT Libraries, assist with the *development and implementation of policies and procedures for bibliographic and authority control,* and supervise planning and process improvements for the CMS department. The candidate will be expected to *perform original and complex adaptive cataloging using RDA, LCSH, LC classification, and metadata descriptors.*

The Catalog Management Librarian will be working across departments and divisions, specifically with the Resource Discovery Librarian (systems), Digital Libraries, Access Services, and Collection Development. This librarian will supervise staff, students, and interns, providing direction and assistance in all unit functions. In the absence of the Head of CMS, may serve as interim manager. UNT librarians hold faculty-equivalent status, and are thus expected to participate in scholarly, professional, and services activities that enhance their departmental responsibilities.

QUALIFICATIONS

Required

- *Master's Degree in Library or Information Science from an ALA-accredited program,* or its international equivalent.
- Successful completion of *cataloging coursework* at the Master's Degree level including *descriptive cataloging, LC Subject Headings and LC Classification.*
- Knowledge *of RDA.*
- Adaptive cataloging experience.

- Metadata descriptor experience.
- Familiarity with an Integrated Library System.
- Proficiency in written and oral communication skills.

Preferred

- *One-year supervisory experience* (staff, students, or interns).
- Experience in acquiring, editing, and *loading files* of vendor-supplied bibliographic records.
- Knowledge of current issues and principles regarding RDA.
- Familiarity with *OCLC Connexion*.
- Familiarity with III Sierra.
- Ability to work without direct supervision.
- Evidence of publishing and/or participation in professional organizations appropriate to the level of appointment.

In order to be considered for this position, the applicant needs to be familiar with RDA, LCSH, LC classification and metadata description. The candidate also must have a MLS and have worked for a year using an integrated library system. The preferred candidate should have some supervisory experience, the ability to load vendor records and a knowledge of the hiring institution's integrated library system.

Now it should be fairly easy for you to go through your résumé or CV and identify your professional experience that is appropriate for this position. Information that is not relevant can be downplayed or eliminated entirely.

RESPONSE TO THE HIRING COMMITTEE

If you are interested in this job, you might write a letter like this:

To the search committee:

I am submitting my CV in response to your posting of the position of catalog management librarian. I have been doing original and copycat cataloging at my institution for a year and a half. In this position I am responsible for the supervision and training of a student worker. Recently, we made the transition from Voyager to the WMS, and I am familiar with both systems. I have taken two classes for credit through our local consortium on the basics of RDA and Dublin Core. I received my MLS from Rutgers University's School of

Communication and Information in 2016, where I completed coursework on metadata for information professionals, emerging technologies, and data management. I very much look forward to hearing from you and having the opportunity to discuss this position further.

Sincerely,
XXX

What if you are interested in this job position, but you are unsure about your qualifications? Take a look at the job advertisement again. You'll notice that the institution has identified as its job pool recent graduates from a LIS program, which means that the committee does not expect candidates to have substantial job experience. If you still feel that your qualifications are shaky, you might want to sign up for a cataloging Webinar, take a short course, or intern at your public library or college in the technical services department to become familiar with the skills you will need.

Here's another advertisement, this time for a school librarian. Notice the minimum qualifications for this position as well as the preferred qualifications.

A HIGH SCHOOL ACADEMY

Founded in 2010 by Instituto del Progreso Latino, a leading community based educational center, the Instituto Health Sciences Career Academy (IHSCA) is dedicated to preparing students for careers in health care, an area that is chronically short of personnel and will have a high demand in the foreseeable future. The school will serve as a bridge to a variety of careers within the health professions. Our students are being prepared to pursue higher education or prepare them to go from the classroom directly into the workplace.

IHSCA's mission is to prepare students for success in competitive colleges and universities while simultaneously providing job readiness certifications in entry-level positions with higher wages at the healthcare sector. We envision our school as an intergenerational community education center, with full integration and participation of faculty, students, staff, parents, and partners in decisions that shape the school's existence.

Job Description

The librarian reports to the assistant principal and works with teachers and other educators to build and strengthen connections between student information and research needs, curricular content, learning outcomes, and information resources. The librarian empowers students to become critical thinkers, enthusiastic readers, skillful researchers, and ethical users of information. Work within the school-wide culture to foster curiosity in student and staff learners by providing a variety of innovative formats to teach, enrich, and expand critical, creative, and independent thinking.

Essential Duties and Responsibilities

- *Promotes reading* in traditional and innovative ways, such as social media, digital media, and print (information, media, visual, digital, and technological literacy)
- *Organizes* and initiates school-aligned *programs* that encourage learning and offer cultural and global opportunities for school community
- Collaborates with teachers (classroom and advisory) in *the design of instructional lessons* integrating appropriate informational literacy and technology skills.
- Assist teachers in *choosing high-quality literature* to supplement and enrich their curricular studies. Student Review Web Page Project (juniors) and the Career Research Google Site Project (seniors), Empower projects
- Develop reading materials to support Career Pathway
- *Hold library orientation sessions* to review library rules and policy, introduction to space layout, Dewey decimal system, library Web site, and time for SRR book check out.
- Promote literature, reinforce reading skills, and encourage independent reading for personal enjoyment in various formats (e.g., print, nonprint, large print, audio, electronic, high-interest/low-level)
- Responsible for *circulation and catalog services*
- Maintain the circulation and cataloging systems
- Responsible for *day-to-day operations* (e.g., reshelving, deselecting materials, evaluating donations, providing ready reference, reference interviews, inventory, reader advisory)
- Develop displays and exhibits to promote reading
- Instruct students in methods for obtaining material not available in their school library (e.g., interlibrary loan, public library, academic library)
- Collaborate with public libraries and encourage students to participate in public library programs (e.g., after-school reading activities, summer reading club, and others)
- Provide book talks, book clubs and promote award-winning books
- Extend the reading experience by suggesting additional titles in a series, or identifying additional works within a genre or works with similar themes
- Offer reading enrichment programming through participation in national and state reading celebrations and initiatives (i.e., Children's Book Week, Teen Read Week, National Library Week, School Library Month, Right to Read Week)
- Identify reading/literacy initiatives available in the community—develop and lead Latino Family Literacy Program and school-wide literacy nights (in collaboration with English Department)

- Ensure there is a collection of reading materials by and about various ethnicities and cultural groups. Extend awareness of gender, culture, and historical perspectives through literature.
- Provide information about school library services, hours of operation, staff, user guides, pathfinders, Internet access, and other available resources
- Demonstrate responsible and ethical usage of library-based technologies.
- Model effective strategies for developing multiple literacies
- Understand copyright, fair use, and licensing of intellectual property, and assisting users with their understanding and observance of the same
- Develop and evaluate the school library program with goals and objectives that are aligned with school goals and priorities
- Use effective management principles, including the supervision of resources and facilities
- Prepare and monitor the school library program budget to support specific program goals
- Ensure that the school library is a teaching and learning environment that is inviting, safe, flexible, and conducive to student learning
- Arrange for flexible scheduling of the school libraries to provide student accessibility to staff and resources at point of need
- Ensure equitable physical access to school library facilities by providing barrier-free, universally designed environments

Qualifications

- *Bachelor's degree, master's in library and information science from an accredited university.*
- *Bilingual, English/Spanish preferred*
- *At least four years teaching experience (is a plus)*
- *Illinois Type 9 certification (is a plus)*
- *Ability to maintain a high sense of confidentiality*
- Reader advisory expertise with diverse understanding of young adult literature
- Able to work with a wide variety of people
- Team player and willing to take on multiple tasks at once and independent worker, requires minimal supervision
- Exceptional organization, leadership, and time-management skills
- Above average "customer" service attitude
- Excellent oral and written communication skills
- Strong telephone skills and ability to maintain composure under pressure
- Dependable and punctual
- Strong project management skills, attention to detail and effective management of multiple projects at one time
- Ability to adhere to deadlines, react to unpredictable events quickly and efficiently, be resourceful, manage conflict and challenges

- *Experience with classification systems (e.g., Dewey Decimal System or Library of Congress Classification System), MARC records, and cataloging practices. Experience with SOAR— integrated library system is a plus*
- *Advanced skills with Microsoft Office, Word, Excel, PowerPoint, and the Internet*

RECOGNIZING WHAT IS NOT SAID BUT IMPLIED

A lengthy solicitation like this is a good example of why it is so important to read through a job advertisement several times to understand what an employer is looking for. The required qualifications are a bachelor's degree, knowledge of cataloging and classification, and a facility with Microsoft Office and the Internet. Preferred qualifications include familiarity with a specific integrated library system, four years of work experience, fluency in Spanish and English, and possession of an Illinois teaching certificate. However, what the search committee is looking for may not be so obvious.

Let's take a look at this particular paragraph:

The librarian reports to the assistant principal and works with teachers and other educators to build and strengthen connections between student information and research needs, curricular content, learning outcomes, and information resources. The librarian empowers students to become critical thinkers, enthusiastic readers, skillful researchers, and ethical users of information. Work within the school-wide culture to foster curiosity in student and staff learners by providing a variety of innovative formats to teach, enrich, and expand critical, creative, and independent thinking.

If these sentences sound familiar, they should; they are based on the guidelines for information literacy established by the American Association of School Librarians (AASL; https://standards.aasl.org).

A strategy might be to review the AASL guidelines, making note of the lesson plans associated with each, as a way of preparing for an interview.

If you read through the advertisement again, you will see that there are two preferred qualifications that are critically important: "bilingual, English/Spanish preferred" and "Illinois Type 9 certification." The latter is a licensure requirement for teaching in the state of Illinois. Since the students at the Health Care Sciences Career Academy, a charter school, are largely Latino immigrants, it would make sense that the new hire is bilingual in Spanish and English. These two "preferred qualifications" might be the deciding factors in receiving a job offer.

Lastly, here is a job announcement for an academic position:

SJSU Information School Announces Assistant Professor Open Position

The School of Information at San José State University is recruiting for a tenure-track assistant professor in the area of Organizational Management and Behavior in Information Professions.

Applicants should have:

- Experience in teaching 100 percent online courses in . . .
- Challenges and critical success factors of information service development
- Strategic long-term management and daily challenges involved in leading and supporting physical and digital library initiatives
- Effective mediation between the users of information and the resources and information systems in specific organizational contexts
- Best practices in library and information service strategic planning
- Performance measures that contribute to the effective development of library and information services

Research interests in at least one of the following:

- *Advocacy and advocacy metrics* in the information professions
- *Decision making* in the information professions
- *Management of globally distributed teams* of information professionals who work in globally distributed online environments—both profit and nonprofit

An earned doctorate must be completed by the time of application.

Applications close on February 14, 2018. Download/read full job description and how to apply.

As you can see this job announcement is different from the previous ones. It lists two equally important requirements, teaching and research. Although it is an open entry-level academic position, which means that no particular kind of subject specialization is needed, the announcement tells you that there actually three preferred areas of concentration: advocacy and advocacy metrics in the information professions, decision making in the information professions, and management of globally distributed teams. You'll notice that the teaching is done entirely online.

THE COVER LETTER

Probably the most significant thing you can do to increase your chances of getting an interview is to write a compelling cover letter. A wise approach is to do as much research as possible on the institution you wish to join, most of which is probably readily available on the Web. If a library committee is conducting the search and you are given the names of the members, see if you can find information about their job responsibilities, scholarship, and interests as well. In framing the cover letter, make sure you read the job advertisement carefully, so that you are able to answer positively and enthusiastically about your qualifications for the position.

Below is a template that could be customized for a librarian applying for an academic library position:

> As the director of a small college library, I successfully developed and implemented an information literacy program that supports our two-year curriculum. Students learn how to use our academic databases and catalog and research skills, such as proper citation and bibliographic annotation. I created a pre- and post-test that is distributed before and after my instructional classes. On average, students show a 25 percent improvement in their information literacy skills on the post-test. My activities also included faculty outreach, reference, and collection development. In addition to initiating our chat service, I trained and supervised a staff of three paraprofessionals to take on this function. I served on the university-wide student advancement committee and chaired the Senate Library Committee.
>
> I am seeking to join a collaborative environment that will allow me to pursue my instructional and reference skills in the service of a multicultural student population, like that of University Y.
>
> Sincerely,
> Xxx

And the reverse—how not to write a cover letter.

> Dear Sir/ Madam,
> I am interested in applying as a librarian at your institution. The fact that I am also working in a similar situation makes me feel comfortable; I share things in common with the rest of the team. I believe that my 20 years in the profession practicing librarianship in a school setting makes me feel confident to apply. If given a chance, I am most willing to relocate. I am hoping that my résumé attached in my application would be suitable to your needs. Rest assured of my dedication and loyalty.
>
> Thank you very much.
> Sincerely,

One of the most important part of the hiring process is checking the applicant's references. If you are applying for a job, you always want to pick someone who knows you well, either as a supervisor or as a colleague. You also want to approach your references first, before listing them as contacts. You should provide them with a copy of the job you are applying for and your most recent CV.

Here is an example of the kind of recommendation you'd like to receive.

August 27, 2014

Human Resources Department
To Whom It May Concern:

Please let me introduce myself. I am the Director of X Library, the public library in Anywhere, USA. X library is a member of our regional consortium. It was in my role as Board Director from 2015 to 2017 that I worked with Ms. Xxx. Ms. Xxx served as the Fiscal Officer of our consortium. In the position she handled budgeting, payroll, and accounts payable. Ms. Xxx was prompt, efficient, and worked well with both the consortium staff and the consortium members. I highly recommend her for this job position and look forward to being contacted as a personal reference.

Let's take for example, the case of Mary, a reference librarian, who is applying for a job in a historical society. She has been asked to talk for 15 or 20 minutes about her experience with genealogical researchers and the skills she will bring to the institution from her current job.

Mary quickly realizes, from the way the request is phrased, that the hiring committee is worried about her lack of experience working with genealogical materials. She also understands that it views her 10 years of experience as a professional librarian as an asset. What she does not know is that the historical society desperately wants to modernize its operations and is looking for someone who might be able to bring order to its archives.

Mary's first steps are to find out as much information about the historical society as she can and about genealogy in general. She visits an old friend, who has retired from a similar position, and asks as many questions as she can, in particular about the needs of researchers and the kind of questions they tended to ask. She goes through her résumé and identifies any past work and volunteer experiences that seems applicable. At the last moment, she decides to prepare a Web guide for the historical society based on two similar guides she found in Springshare's Community Lib-Guides database.[2]

It was the last part of the presentation, when Mary presented her Web guide, along with 10 years of work experience and her friendly personality, that convinced the committee to hire her.

If you are asked to give a presentation, the audience generally will be given an evaluation form when you finish that looks something like this:

CANDIDATE EVALUATION FORM

Name of candidate:

Strengths:

Weaknesses:

Presentation rating: Excellent Good Satisfactory Unsatisfactory

Please describe your opinion of the candidate's presentation in terms of clarity and content.

Does the candidate have the relevant job skills to fill this position? Please describe why you think so.

Do you feel the candidate is a positive fit for the library? Y _____ N _____

Additional comments _____

If you are asked to give a presentation, keep in mind that no matter how friendly the audience seems, they are still evaluating you. Be pleasant and polite. Don't be intimidated by hostile individuals who seem to be questioning your ability. Confidence and prior preparation should be able to get you through the interview with flying colors.

CHAPTER TAKEAWAY

Applying for a job position is essentially like running a campaign. There are milestones that you need to pass in order to reach your objective. The first one is an understanding of the job requirements and preparing a well-written CV and cover letter. The second is having a successful job interview and, if appropriate, giving a talk or presentation on a topic related to librarianship. The last is making a good impression during interviews and following up with a thank-you letter to the committee or individual who meets with you.

NOTES

1. "Career Site," Office of the Provost—UNT, n.d., https://facultyjobs.unt.edu.

2. LibGuides Community. https://community.libguides.com/.

TEN

Writing for Students Who Seek a Degree, LIS Professors, and Academic Librarians on the Tenure Track

MLIS STUDENTS

One of the defining features of librarianship is its emphasis on continuing education. Most of us are drawn to the profession precisely for that reason—we love the process of continuous inquiry and learning. We are a profession of praxis, and in order to keep up with developments in our field, we attend and present at conferences, participate in Webinars and in-house training sessions and read the professional literature. These are all activities you will engage in throughout your career as an informational professional, and many of you are doing these activities right now in graduate school.

Librarianship also is distinguished by the diversity of experiences professionals bring to the field. Although many students enroll in a MLIS program directly after college, a substantial number of students are second career professionals. Regardless of whether you are just out of college or embarking on a new career, you will spend much of your time writing papers and completing assignments in your MLIS program and the education will be just as challenging and exhilarating, no matter what stage you are at in your career.

In graduate school you will learn how to present material in formats that are standard for the profession—for example, using PowerPoint for presentations and APA style for your papers. Most likely you will be exposed to many Web-based tools and products like WordPress, Lib-Guides, and Camtasia and programing language like Python and Perl that will enable you to do your job more efficiently.

Most importantly you will learn how to write as an academic. You'll need to become familiar with the professional vocabulary of our field and understand how the library literature is constructed. Paper assignments are the most frequent kind of academic writing done in graduate school. Because you might have seven or eight papers to complete in one semester, it is easy to become overwhelmed by competing demands on your time. Here are some observations, drawn from many years of experience as both a teacher and a student that may make these assignments easier.

OBSERVATION #1 READ THE CLASS SYLLABUS. THEN READ IT AGAIN.

The syllabus is a contract between you and the professor. It describes what you and the professor are required to do over the course of the semester. Your LIS professors may be adjuncts brought in teach a particular course or several courses simultaneously or they may be scholars for whom research is their principal agenda item. No matter what their background, your professors have set objectives that they would like you, the student, to achieve. These are clearly stated in the syllabus. Let's say, for example, that you are enrolled in a course on social media. Before beginning a writing assignment, you'll want to read the course syllabus carefully and find out what those objectives are and how the professor defines an A, B, or C grade. If your professor is an adjunct, he or she was probably brought in because of his or her exemplary work as practitioner. This course, therefore, may focus on skills acquisition. If your professor is a tenured or tenure-track faculty member, most likely he or she is teaching in his or her area of research. In the case of both the adjunct and the tenure-track professor, you may decide to go a step further and read what they have published in the professional literature. This will give you an understanding of their research and may help you formulate the approach you want to take in a writing assignment. Does this sound familiar? It should. It is very much like steps you go through in preparing a job application (see Chapter 9).

OBSERVATION #2 GRAD SCHOOL PAPERS SHOULD BE AS JARGON FREE AS POSSIBLE.

It is always better to write in simple, clear prose. As I've tried to stress throughout this book, clarity should be the rule, not the exception, in professional writing. This also holds true for all your written work in graduate school—the threads you respond to in your online course management system and the assignments and papers you write. In the template method, you build your ideas on an existing foundation. This gives you extraordinary flexibility. If you don't like the way your thesis flows, you can break a document into its components, paragraphs. We can move these from one part of the document to another, to see where they make the most sense, and then find the right transitional phrases to bridge the gap between them.

Here is a deconstructed paragraph from an editorial on open access. Can you put the sentences back together in an order that makes sense?

> Today, the value of information is precisely the opposite, a result its sheer volume and the myriad ways it can be repackaged and sold.
>
> Unlike our clientele, the majority of academic librarians did not and do not participate in a gaming culture or (except peripherally) in online social networking.
>
> One of the most provocative mantras of the past few years, "Information wants to be free," bears examining because it is at odds with so many of our professional values—the belief in the right to privacy, the commitment to provide accurate and verifiable information, a respect for copyright law, and a wariness toward the commercialization of information.
>
> Part of this is due to generational differences.
>
> We grew up in a society in which information was valued for its scarcity and more often its exclusivity.[1]

HERE IS THE TEXT IN ITS RIGHT ORDER:

One of the most provocative mantras of the past few years, "Information wants to be free," bears examining because it is at odds with so many of our professional values—the belief in the right to privacy, the commitment to provide accurate and verifiable information, a respect for copyright law, and a wariness toward the commercialization of information.

Part of this is due to generational differences. Unlike our clientele, the majority of academic librarians did not and do not participate in a gaming culture or (except peripherally) in online social networking. We grew up in a society in which information was valued for its scarcity ad more often its exclusivity. Today, the value of information is precisely the opposite, a result of its sheer volume and the myriad ways it can be repackaged and sold.

OBSERVATION #3 START WITH A TEMPLATE.

Let's say that your assignment is to prepare an exhaustive annotated bibliography on the topic of digital literacy and its impact on a particular user group. This kind of search is similar to one you might make as a corporate or reference librarian.

A simple template for an annotated bibliography might look like this.

AN ANNOTATED BIBLIOGRAPHY

Parameters of project
Citation 1
Descriptive paragraph (annotation)
Citation 2
Descriptive paragraph (annotation) . . .
Concluding remarks

For your own project, you might begin by establishing a definition of digital literacy and then listing examples:

TITLE OF PROJECT

Definition of Digital Literacy: Include definitions from a variety of disciplines.

Create format headings—for example, print and e-articles, blogs, twitter feeds, print and eBooks, government documents . . .

Citation 1

Descriptive paragraph (annotation)

Citation 2
Descriptive paragraph (annotation) . . .
Create headings for core topics—names and addresses of experts in the field,
examples of how the approach to digital literacy has changed over time, key texts
Citation 1
Descriptive paragraph (annotation)
Citation 2
Descriptive paragraph (annotation) . . .
Concluding remarks

DO A SKILLS INVENTORY

In a LIS program, students are often asked to write a paper about an aspect of librarianship. This can be frustrating for many students, who think that they don't know enough to write or speak knowledgeably about a profession they have not yet entered. That's simply not true.

A self-assessment of your abilities is called doing a skills inventory. If you are a work-study student at the library, what kind of experiences— handling circulation, shelving, interlibrary loan—do you know well enough to write about? Did you enter the profession from a related field, like publishing? If so, can you draw comparisons between the two? Don't worry if feel anxious at the moment; as you transition into your first job, there will be many opportunities for building your writing skills, including conference posters, in-house presentations, and seminar proceedings.

LIS PROFESSORS AND ACADEMIC LIBRARIANS ON THE TENURE TRACK

Academia is a special kind of work environment because, well, it is academia. Even though U.S. universities often resemble a business in the way they are administered, they still retain many characteristics of the early European universities they are descended from. Graduate faculty come to the profession believing that they will mentor and train students much in the same way their predecessors did, going as far back as the Classic Age. Think of Plato, for example, who was Socrates's student and Aristotle, who was the student of Plato. LIS professors are generally hired on the tenure track. The adage "publish or perish" is very real for these faculty, who only have a certain amount of time to achieve tenure. As the result, a large part of their time is spent applying for grants, doing research, and publishing. These requirements should be laid out in departmental guidelines for tenure or in the university faculty guide.

About half of all librarians at colleges and universities in the United States have faculty status. With it comes the possibility of getting tenure. Librarians who hold faculty status or similar administrative rank at a university or college do the same kind of professional writing as other librarians. They author reports and memos, prepare job descriptions, and write recommendation letters. However, unlike school librarians and public librarians, their professional advancement depends upon scholarly research and publication, similar to that of LIS academics. This research is also expected to be driven by a cohesive scholarly agenda. So, for example, if you are an instructional librarian, you probably would focus on research involving information literacy, and if you are an archivist, your focus most likely would be on a topic like metadata or oral history. Very rarely do librarians write on topics not related to their profession, although they will write on a subject specialty if they have a degree in another discipline.

As defined by the American Association of University Professors (AAUP), "a tenured appointment is an indefinite appointment that can be terminated only for cause or under extraordinary circumstances such as financial exigency and program discontinuation." [2] Tenure is often awarded between the fifth and seventh year of employment. If you are an academic professor or librarian who has been hired on the tenure track, you would do well to plan out a strategy right from the start. Make sure this includes long-term quantitative goals (e.g., I need to write four articles and serve on five committees before I come up for tenure.) and an annual plan that includes some kind of qualitative evaluation (e.g., What are my job responsibilities and am I meeting them? What is my research agenda and is it developing in a meaningful way?).

Most tenure-track candidates have to submit documentation of their activities to their rank and tenure committee each year before they come up for promotion. This documentation is generally called a tenure packet or a dossier. In it, the applicant provides evidence of professional effectiveness, his or her research agenda and publications, and service to the university and larger community. Most likely, the year before you come up for tenure, you will complete your dossier and submit it to your chair. Your application will be read by your department and faculty in other divisions of the university. That is why it is important that your application be jargon free and clearly written. A faculty member in the Biosciences, for example, won't be knowledgeable about library research, and the tenure applicant will have to work hard to make his or her application understandable. You may want to get colleagues in other disciplines to read through your dossier for clarity.

All this should be specified in the university faculty guide or a similar document. These guidelines will vary from school to school, but most often the requested documentation includes internal and external recommendations of the candidate, physical copies of his or her publications, and a CV. Often, the applicant submits a personal statement as well.

Here is an excerpt from a personal statement by an academic librarian who successfully achieved tenure at her university:

I am liaison and subject specialist for the sciences (departments of Biology & Microbiology, Chemistry & Biochemistry, Physics, Mathematics and Environmental Studies) and Health Sciences (Athletic Training, Occupational Therapy, Physician Assistant, Physical Therapy, Speech Language Pathology, and the PhD in Health Sciences). I am also liaison for the department of Sociology, Anthropology & Social Work. In addition to providing formal and informal instruction sessions and research assistance to faculty, classes, and students in my liaison areas, I provide general reference service at the reference desk, by appointment, online, via e-mail, live chat and telephone, and through opportunistic encounters in the library and around campus. Last year I taught 50 library instruction classes (including English 1201 and 1202) and had nine individual research appointments. I also met individually with 11 students in Anthropology of Consciousness, a course in which I was embedded in spring 2017.

My liaison, instruction, and reference work demonstrate professional effectiveness in relation to the University Libraries' interpretation of Boyer's "knowledge responsibly applied" umbrella by "communicating knowledge effectively" to students, faculty, and other members of the community. My work as a subject specialist includes collection development (developing our physical book collection, eBook collections, and other online resources) and disseminating information about library resources to those in my liaison areas. I believe I offer "expert knowledge of materials and resources in [my] areas of responsibility" and beyond. My major contributions to the University Libraries' goals and objectives are. . . .

As you can see, the librarian, who holds a PhD, chose to emphasize her flexibility and willingness to set up research consultations with students. She referenced Boyer's theory of learning because it was the basis her school's approach to teaching and learning. Lastly, she discussed how her efforts contributed to the University Libraries' strategic plan.

If you are either a tenure-track faculty member or a tenure-track academic librarian, you will want to review the dossier of a colleague in your department or library, who has already achieved tenure. Most likely, this dossier will include copies of his or her publications, teaching evaluations, recommendation letters from faculty has served on committees with, and possibly an external review of his or her scholarship. If you decide to use his or her dossier as a template for your own tenure application, I'd suggest you start by reviewing your own documentation to make sure it supports your narrative. If it doesn't, remove and reorganize the dossier so that the progression of documents made sense. Next, I'd create a template of the application itself and identify the areas that needed information. As you've most likely realized, I would not even begin to write my opening statement until I had assembled all my data.

Longwood University was founded in 1839 and has a rich history as a normal school, a state teachers' college. Although it has grown into a small, comprehensive university with a strong curriculum in liberal arts and sciences, an emphasis on quality teaching is still evident in the promotion and tenure (P&T) process. Secondly, Longwood's stated mission is to prepare citizen leaders, and this mission and the expectation of faculty service are also emphasized in the P&T process. The third prong is scholarship, and along with the expectation for exceptional teaching and service is the expectation of research and writing. The P&T process described here applies to faculty members in the Master of Education in School Librarianship program, housed in the Department of Education and Special Education in the College of Education and Human Services.

Expectations and Requirements for Promotion and Tenure

From Assistant to Associate—University Requirements:

According to the University *Faculty Policies and Procedures Manual* (FPPM; 135–136, 138–139), promotion and tenure are based on the following criteria:

"a.   Possession of the recognized terminal degree.

b.   Quality teaching, scholarship and service as defined by University and departmental standards. . . .

c.   Evidence of a record of scholarly activity recognized by disciplinary peers outside the institution, including one peer-reviewed contribution relevant to the discipline, and potential for further professional and scholarly growth. Peer-reviewed contribution means notable creative work and/or notable professional publication or achievement recognized by disciplinary peers outside the institution."

From Assistant to Associate—Department Requirements (FPPM, 179–181):

Teaching effectiveness is demonstrated through evidence of content knowledge, presentation of material, assessment and evaluation of student learning, and creation of a positive learning environment. Service includes such activities as serving on or chairing department, college, or university committees; sponsoring student organizations; participating in academic student recruitment; advising students; and developing new courses, course content, or programs.

In the area of scholarship, "for tenure and/or promotion to Associate Professor, a candidate must demonstrate evidence of continuing scholarly activity, which must include at least one (1) peer-reviewed publication and four (4) other acceptable examples of scholarly activities (three other acceptable examples if the peer-reviewed publication is a book) . . . within the probationary period." Other scholarly activities include, but are not limited to, submitting a peer-reviewed grant proposal; serving as a peer-reviewer for manuscripts, chapters, books, etc.; serving as editor for a book, book series, or publication; conducting original research and disseminating information at professional meetings and/or conferences.

From Associate to Full—University Requirements:

From *FPPM* (139):

Professor—"In addition to meeting the general criteria for promotion, the candidate shall have produced creative work, professional publication or achievement, or quality research judged significant by peers outside the institution. The candidate must have completed eleven years of full-time tenure-track college teaching, including five years of full-time tenure-track college teaching (or academic librarianship in the case of librarians) at the rank of associate professor, prior to beginning the application process with the time table. . . ."

From Associate to Full—Department Requirements (*FPPM*, 180):

"For promotion to Full Professor, a candidate must demonstrate evidence of continuing scholarly activity, which must include at least two (2) peer-reviewed publications and six (6) other acceptable examples of scholarly activities (five other acceptable examples if one of the peer-reviewed publications is a book) . . . within the preceding five-year period."

Promotion and Tenure Process

From Assistant to Associate

At Longwood, initial P&T is a six-year process, with tenure and promotion from assistant to associate professor granted concurrently. Expectations for the process and timelines for year one, years two through five, and year six are clearly outlined in the university's *FPPM*. During year one, faculty members create a professional portfolio that documents their teaching, service, scholarship, and plan for continued professional growth. During years two through five, the portfolio is updated to add current documents and evidence. During year six, the faculty member "goes up" for promotion and tenure.

Each year, the first tier of review occurs at the department level and is completed concurrently by the Department Chair and the Department P&T Committee. The P&T Committee is composed of three tenured faculty members in the department, elected to serve by their department peers. Recommendations for progression through the P&T process are based on review of all aspects of the faculty member's professional portfolio and observations of classroom teaching. P&T Committee members and the Department Chair complete separate reviews and recommendations. The second review tier is with the Dean of the College of Education and Human Services. Recommendations from the P&T Committee, Department Chair, and College Dean then go to the Provost and Vice President for Academic Affairs (PVPAA). From the PVPAA recommendations go to the President and then to the University Board of Visitors for final approval. Excellence in teaching, service to the university, increasing scholarship, and ongoing professional growth are expected each year.

Personal Experience in Promotion and Tenure Process

As I started the P&T process, a very wise and seasoned department chair gave me valuable advice. He told me to strive to publish at least one "something" each year, preferably in a peer-reviewed journal, but not to discount prestigious practitioner journals for publication opportunities as well. He also encouraged me to submit conference presentation proposals each year, preferably at the national or state level.

I took his advice as I worked through the P&T process and, in the five years preceding my going up for tenure and promotion to associate professor during the 2008–2009 academic year, I had three articles published in *Library Media Connection*, two in *Multimedia and Internet @ Schools*, one in *Teacher Librarian* (peer-reviewed), and one in *School Library Media Research* (peer-reviewed). I also published two books, *Leverage Your Library Program to Help Raise Test Scores* (Linworth, 2003) and *Your Library Goes Virtual* (Linworth, 2007). During this time I presented 18 sessions at state conferences and three sessions at national conferences. I earned tenure and was promoted to associate professor for the 2009–2010 academic year.

Over the next six years, as I worked toward promotion from associate to full professor, I had five articles published in *Knowledge Quest*, one in the *Delta Kappa Gamma Bulletin*, one in *Library Media Connection*, one in *Principal Leadership*, and one in *School Library Monthly*; I also had three peer-reviewed articles published, one in the *Journal of Education for Library and Information Science* and two in *School Library Research*. During the same time period, I presented 28 sessions at state conferences and seven sessions at national conferences. I was promoted to full professor for the 2015–2016 academic year.

At Longwood University the expectation is for excellence—in teaching, in service, and in scholarship—and for continued learning, professional growth, and contributions to the field.[3]

Audrey P. Church, PhD

Assembling a tenure dossier can take six months or more. Early on you will need to create some kind of filing system for your supporting documentation. The university where I work requires the following evidence:

- Evidence of excellence in teaching
- Evidence of university and community service
- Evidence of publications and research in progress
- Correspondence, recommendations, and miscellanea

In preparation for writing the application, I would think through each of the categories to decide what evidence would be the most useful.

Evidence of Teaching
Number of classes taught in the proceeding five years
Letters from students and teachers

University and Community Service
Thank-you and acknowledgment letters

Evidence of Scholarship
Acceptance letters from university presses, physical copies of journals, and conference papers; abstracts from poster sessions

---

Here is an example of the requirements for tenure and promotion to associate professor for faculty teaching at Syracuse University.[4]

TENURE/PROMOTION SUMMARY DOSSIER FOR VICE CHANCELLOR AND PROVOST

Please assemble the following items in this order:

1. Outline of Professional Experience (Form A)
2. Candidate Statement (Form A)
3. Committee and department (if applicable) recommendations, votes and analysis, including:
   a. Departmental evaluative summary about the quality and quantity of (1) the candidate's scholarly production, including specific comments about refereed publications that include (for monographs) the suitability of the press, how well known in the field and (for journals) rating in the field and acceptance rate; and the work's impact on the field; and/ or (2) creative work produced and the quality and suitability of the

venues in which the work is presented and the impact on the audience and genre of production; and/or (3) public scholarship and engagement projects, including comments on the project's significance, and its impact on the publics, communities, industries or other partners or audiences.

b. Departmental evaluative summary about the quality and quantity of teaching and other instructional contributions, include effectiveness of classroom teaching, course/curriculum development, and advising.

c. Departmental evaluative summary about the quality and quantity of service to the department, school/college, the University, the profession, or the public.

d. For promotion to full professor, evidence of significant accomplishment and impact.

4. Copies of 5–7 outside letters of review solicited and

a. List of all names solicited with information that describes the person and the qualifications that make him/her especially appropriate as a reference. Include the reason(s) given for a solicited reviewer declining letter(s)

b. Copies of solicitation letter(s)

5. School/College evaluative recommendations, votes and analysis (see above)

6. Dean's analysis and recommendation

Writing and Research for Promotion and Tenure

When I first arrived at my current institution and department, I obtained a copy of their promotion and tenure (P&T) document as well as the university's P&T policy. The university policy is quite broad and states only the very basic criteria for P&T of faculty. It states that each department sets its own criteria for P&T of faculty. The department's P&T policy is more specific about the criteria upon which faculty will be evaluated and gives examples of means by which faculty may demonstrate the achievement of each criteria. Like other P&T policies that I have encountered, my department's policy is careful to avoid prescribing particular activities and amounts of those activities by which a faculty member is guaranteed to achieve tenure. I have always sensed that P&T policies are written this way in order to allow faculty promotion committees, department chairs, deans, and so on, that is those who are making P&T recommendations and decisions, the broadest possible latitude in those decisions. It was not until I began to reflect on this manuscript that I realized that this broadness in P&T policies also gives individual faculty members flexibility to create a customized plan for achieving P&T. However, having said that, I can also see in hindsight that this is exactly what I did.

At the time I joined their faculty, the academic department in which I work required each untenured faculty member to submit a portfolio and narrative describing their accomplishments in the areas of teaching, research, and service at the beginning of each fall semester beginning in their second year. The portfolio and narrative are reviewed by the same committee of tenured faculty who review P&T applications. The committee provides feedback each year in the form of a letter to the dean recommending to reappointment (or not). The dean also provides feedback each year in the form of a letter to the provost recommending reappointment. In preparing the subsequent year's portfolio and narrative, I made sure to address the previous year's recommendations and provide artifacts (copies of publications, invitations to review, etc.) as evidence of having followed through on them.

This system has advantages and disadvantages, although for me the advantages outweighed the disadvantages. The main disadvantage was the amount of time required to put together a portfolio and narrative. This is mitigated by the benefit of having a collection of artifacts and reflective narratives for each year that I would have to address in my full, sixth year, P&T portfolio. In addition to that advantage, I found it extremely helpful to receive some annual, written, guidance from the senior, tenured faculty and the dean on my progress toward P&T. Their recommendations were always offered in the form of constructive criticism and with the intention to help me to improve as a researcher and writer.

Having to produce an annual portfolio for evaluation forced me to give priority to keeping my curriculum vitae and research agenda statements up-to-date. In retrospect, writing and revising a research agenda was one of the most helpful activities to meeting P&T requirements. I kept (and still keep) a journal of research ideas, problems, and questions that are of interest to me but that I do not currently have time to pursue. This is also where I make note of progress on the current research and writing projects that I am pursuing. Faculty have a lot of freedom in terms of how they spend their time, but that makes it easier to overcommit to projects, research and otherwise, and to deviate from those activities that lead most directly to the goal of P&T. Keeping a research journal and using it to update a research agenda statement was very helpful for me in terms of carefully choosing writing and research projects and staying on a track that led to P&T.

Next to keeping a research journal and updating my research agenda statement annually, collaborations and research partnerships were the most important step I took to meeting my department's P&T requirements. I came to my tenure track position with some research and publications already underway, mainly from my dissertation. In my first two years as a faculty member, I built on and updated that work, but I also started work on a topic that had captured my interest during the last years of my doctoral studies that I had put aside in order to complete my dissertation. I approached this topic by asking myself, "What about this topic would practicing librarians would be interested in?" The topic was altmetrics, and the approach was to explore their usefulness to academic librarians' work to develop their collections.

I did some library research on the topic and during my second year on the tenure track, I gave a couple of peer-reviewed presentations on it. During the course of this, I made a connection with a librarian-turned-vendor who was seeking a partner for a survey of academic librarians on their familiarity with and use of altmetrics. My research partner and I, along with my research assistant, conducted the survey and spent the following two years analyzing the survey results, presenting, and publishing them. My research assistant graduated, took a position as an academic librarian, and continued as the third member of this research and writing team. Each of us took the lead on writing reports on a portion of our research results for peer-reviewed presentation and publication. As a result of our collaborative research and writing as a team during the past four years, we have given seven peer-reviewed presentations, presented two peer-reviewed conference proceedings papers, and published two peer-reviewed articles based on our work, an accomplishment that would have been nearly impossible for me to accomplish as a solo researcher working at an institution where teaching is faculty's primary focus.

A third key activity that was an important factor in my meeting my department's P&T requirements was learning to work with a research assistant. This sounds straightforward, but turns out to be rather complicated. For instance, accepting a research assistant comes with the responsibility for filling a certain amount of this person's time, 10 to 20 hours per week at my current institution. This requires a certain amount of planning, preparation, teaching, guiding, and evaluating of the research assistant's work, things that are not always convenient and sometimes compete with other deadlines for my time. On the other hand, having a research assistant and needing to attend to these things also has a way of moving a research project forward, when it might otherwise rate a lesser amount of my attention in the face of activities with harder deadlines like class preparation and grading. I realize that this will not be the case for everyone, but it is the case at my current institution where teaching is the primary focus for faculty.

Because peer-reviewed presentations are valued in my department's P&T guidelines, almost equivalently to peer-reviewed publications, I did a lot of presenting in the first years of my journey along the tenure track. However, with a change in leadership at my department came a change in unwritten expectations for the amounts of research and publication faculty were doing; more publications were expected. That caused me to change tactics; I turned more of my attention to writing and began to focus on presenting at conferences that would result in a publication (conference proceedings).

When it comes to writing, there are several things that come to mind as things I have done specifically in order to make writing to meet P&T requirements less of a challenge (in addition to working with collaborators). Occasionally, I have been sought out as a peer reviewer of others' work in my areas of expertise. The more reviewing work I do, the better I become at accepting reviewer comments and constructive criticisms of my own writing in the spirit in which they are offered: as ways to make my writing and research better. What I still struggle with is the some-times-short turnaround time in which publishers ask for author copy-edits. It always seems to come at the busiest possible time and with the expectation that I will drop everything and work on it.

Another lesson learned about writing and research is stopping to reflect on how I could have done something better. For example, early on in my altmetrics research, my team and I conducted a survey, but we did not write the questions in a way that made the responses easy to analyze using inferential statistics. Had we taken more time to be sure that we asked our survey questions so that we obtained results that met the assumptions of statistical tests, our results would have carried more weight with our readers and been more generalizable. But, that lesson also brought me to the realization that it is important to continue to find and take opportunities to learn and grow as a writing and researcher. For me, finding new books on those topics (writing and researching), learning from my students, and learning from observing others (what to do and what not to do) are the ways in which I have made a conscious effort to evolve and improve as a researcher and writer.

Which brings me back around to writing specifically in my P&T portfolio. My academic journey has included opportunities to learn about and participate in assessment for the purpose of accreditation. Because of that, when it came time to write the narrative portions of my P&T portfolio, it made a certain amount of sense to me to approach the task as a self-assessment. I broke down the criteria for achiev-ing P&T described in my departments' P&T guidelines and addressed each one in the appropriate section of my narrative, including a self-rating and referring to evi-dence and artifacts that demonstrated my achievement. As I have said, this seemed perfectly natural to me, so it came as a bit of a shock and surprise when the chair of my department's P&T committee shared with me that, while the approach I had chosen was fine for the current P&T committee, this had not always been the case in my department. There was a time when it was very much frowned upon to include any sort of self-rating or self-assessment in a P&T portfolio narrative. What I take away from that experience and would share with those coming up the tenure track behind me is that it is very important to talk to tenured faculty about (unwrit-ten) expectations, look at their portfolios, if possible, and ask them why they took the approach they did, and understand the culture and expectations, that is, the context in which you are writing.

Research and writing are, naturally, at the center of meeting tenure and promo-tion requirements, no matter the institution. My experience has taught me to know what is expected, written and unwritten; have a plan and work steadily on it; and seek out feedback. If you are lucky enough to have official channels for feedback, great, but if not, it is worth the effort to seek it out from those who are interpreting the requirements and making decisions. Seek out collaborators for research and writing, accept and make positive use of feedback and criticism, not only from peers and mentors, but also from reviewers and editors. Take time to make the best use of research assistants and stop to reflect, return to the planned path, and change the plan if necessary.

Librarians at research institutions more frequently serve as administrators rather than faculty, but their ranks in service are similar. For example, librarians on the P&T track typically have the rankings of instructor, assistant professor, associate professor, and full professor; academic library administrators who hold continuing appointment might and have the equivalent ranks of librarian I, II, III, and IV. Guidelines for promotion for academic librarians should be found in your university faculty guide or an equivalent document.

Below are the promotion guidelines for librarians at the University of Kansas and Arizona State University. Notice in particular the emphasis on developing a consistent record of research and scholarship. At the University of Kansas, librarians have faculty status; at Arizona State University they do not.

UNIVERSITY OF KANSAS GUIDELINES

Assistant Librarian

Persons being considered for appointment at this rank may or may not be required to have any professional library experience but should be well-qualified to practice librarianship and demonstrate evidence of potential achievement in librarianship, research, and service that contributes to the mission of the Libraries, the University, and the profession. Appointees shall normally remain in this rank for a minimum of five years before promotion to Associate

Librarian. Appointees may remain at this rank for a maximum of six years before mandated review for award of tenure and promotion. This is not a tenurable rank. This rank is equivalent to

Assistant Professor.

ARIZONA STATE UNIVERSITY LIBRARIES GUIDELINES FOR PROMOTION

Library or Academic unit level: the administrator may provide an oral statement of the strengths and weaknesses of the case to the candidate based on the reviews at the library or academic unit level; the candidate may choose to withdraw from further consideration at this point.

College level: the supervising dean/university librarian may provide an oral statement of the strengths and weaknesses of the case to the candidate based on the reviews at the college level; the candidate may choose to withdraw from further consideration at this point.

University level: no notification is made by the university committee.

Final decision: the final decision regarding the award of promotion is made through written notification to the candidate by the president.

PROFESSIONAL AND SCHOLARLY LITERATURE

Although LIS faculty and academic librarians must publish if they hold a tenure-track position, many librarians, who are not employed in academia, choose to do research as well. A primary motivation is their desire to engage in a dialogue with the community about their research. For most of this book, we have spoken about professional writing as the writing librarians do as part of their daily job responsibilities—memos, reports, and so forth. In academia, professional literature has a different meaning. It refers to nonpeer-reviewed publications. Peer review means that an article or book manuscript is submitted to an editor, who then refers it to two or more individuals who are knowledgeable about that particular subject to review. The author's name and affiliation are not known to the reader. This kind of evaluation also is called a "blind review." The editor uses the reviewers' comments to guide her decision to accept or reject the article, or she may ask that the article be revised and resubmitted. In Syracuse's requirements for tenure, you will notice that the first paragraph deals with the candidate's scholarship, including the inclusion of "the quality and quantity of (1) the candidate's scholarly production, including specific comments about refereed publications that include (for monographs) the suitability of the press, how well known in the field and (for journals) rating in the field and acceptance ate; and the work's impact on the field."

Peer-reviewed journals have the *highest citation factor* among all journal publications. A citation factor refers to the number of times an article is cited by another researcher. A journal with a *high impact factor* has a significant number of its articles cited in other publications. An author's reputation is in large part based on the number of citations he or she receives. To find out more about journal citation, you can consult databases like Science Citation Index or Scopus.

The differences between academic and professional literature are no longer as apparent as they once were. The reason is that most researchers now go to the Web first to find information. In our field, open-access publishing is encouraged, as is depositing copies of published work in e-repositories. Open access means that readers can access an online journal without being a subscriber. Either the publisher requires the author or his institution to pay a fee to cover part of the cost of publishing the work, or the work is simply uploaded with the cost absorbed by the host institution, usually a professional society or a university. Open-access journals have had the most success in the sciences, primarily because so much of scientific research is funded by the U.S. federal government. In 2013, the Office of Science and Technology mandated that this research by available for public access. Open access has opened the door for other changes like open peer review, which means that anyone who has access to an online draft of an article can give comments. As a beginning writer, the easiest way to get published is to submit an article into a professional publication. This changing environment will probably affect the kind of articles librarians write and how they are distributed in the future.

PROFESSIONAL LITERATURE

Professional literature is written by experts in the field, but it is done from a practitioner's perspective. Editorials, experience-based articles, annotated Webliographies, and book reviews are all considered professional literature. An example of this kind of publication the is nonpeer-reviewed *College & Research Library News*. Another example is the newsletter, *Against the Grain,* which reports on acquisitions librarianship. I've included some scenarios below of how you might accomplish that and how you could take this opportunity to advance your career.

SCENARIO I

Jane is an instructional librarian at a community college. She has worked in the field for a little under five years. She sees an announcement on a listserv that a well-known journal is looking for book reviewers and applies for the position. The journal sends her a new monograph on the fundamentals of instructional librarianship to review. In reading the book, she becomes interested in the author's approach to student learning and asks her department chair if she can contribute an article to an educational blog about student retention. The attention the posting gets brings her back in touch with a former professor from her LIS school. He encourages her to submit a literature review on student learning to a peer-reviewed journal where he serves on the editorial board.

Result: Jane has begun to develop expertise and a reputation within the field. She also has acquired a mentor.

SCENARIO II

John is the coordinator of school media services in his district. While at the annual School Librarians Conference in his state, he becomes interested in research presented by the keynote speaker on the correlation between frequent library use and student achievement. Because he is an administrator in a large, ethnically diverse district, John wonders how these results are affected by the variables of race and socioeconomic class. He reads the literature suggested by the speaker, and he thinks about how it applies to his own experience. John writes a letter to the editor of *American Libraries* on the topic of student library use and diversity, which is published. John shows the responses to the letter to the superintendent of schools, who encourages him to do his own research and meet with the school board. His report is distributed at a future school board meeting.

Result: John is now considered an up-and-coming expert in this area and an advocate for the district's school library programs. He has been tasked with representing his school district at state-wide meetings.

SCENARIO III

Robert is an assistant professor at a mid-sized university, who is applying for tenure in four years. He does a series of workshops and conference presentations on one of his areas of expertise: cataloging and metadata for the Web. He sends a survey to individuals who have left business cards at his presentations and receives feedback from his peers. He uses this feedback as the basis of a report for his regional journal. He then writes an analysis of current practices in the field for a national refereed journal.

Result: Robert now has scholarly publications and conference presentations that he can add to his tenure packet.

WHERE DO YOU FIND YOUR IDEAS?

When you are just starting out, whether you are a graduate student, a new librarian, or a new faculty member, it is often difficult to decide what to write about. Just remember, ours is a field of praxis. Examine your job skills and responsibilities and ask yourself whether something you do, such as supervising or mentoring staff, teaching, or negotiating licenses can form the basis of an article or presentation. Take a look at anything you've written for work or in a professional setting and see whether it can be turned into a larger piece or help advance your career. I have a colleague who recently made a lateral career move. For many years she had been an area studies librarian, a field that was slowly becoming marginalized. She did a skills inventory and realized that the knowledge she possessed about international copyright law was a skill that few people possessed. She refocused her research and is now a copyright expert at a major international publishing house.

Information professionals frequently present research in progress at conferences as a way of testing out their ideas through a poster session, panel discussion, round table, tech session, or a conference paper. They also will take what they've learned on the job and offer workshops to the community.

Another way to get started writing is to organize or join a writing group. With all the different communication technology available, it is possible to get together with colleagues anywhere in the world through Slack, Skype, WebEx, or another program. Or you can get together the old-fashioned way and find a time in person to discuss a work in progress. Sometimes the best writing groups are the ones composed of faculty from a variety of academic disciplines. This allow you to get an outside and often honest perspective on your work and also may spark ideas that you might never have had otherwise.

PEER-REVIEWED LITERATURE

Let's look at a basic template for an academic article, and see whether we can turn its inherent rigidity to our advantage. Our topic is the use of Google Glass in a community college library. As you can, see the template consists of eight sections:

A TEMPLATE FOR A PEER-REVIEWED ARTICLE

Abstract
Introduction
Literature Review
Methodology
Findings
Discussion
Conclusion
References

Let's start by filling the tasks needed to complete each section and the order in which they should be handled.

A PEER-REVIEWED ARTICLE

Abstract

To be written before you submit to a journal. The abstract is a summary of your findings

Introduction

To be written after you have completed your findings.

Literature review

To be done first
Tasks: discovery-layer searches; individual database searches (e.g., educational, library, technology-specific) as well as Google Scholar
Keywords: Google Glass, wearable technology, student usage; community college libraries

Methodology section

To be done second
Tasks: define focus groups; write survey, pretest, conduct focus-group interviews, and distribute surveys

Findings

To be done after methodology is completed and results are analyzed

Discussion

To be done after findings are completed

Conclusion

To be done after findings are completed

References

To be done throughout
Tasks: review appropriate style guide. Use bibliographic software or other citation tools to keep citations in order.

TYPES OF PEER-REVIEWED LITERATURE

An empirical study is a study in which a researcher collects and analyzes primary data.

A survey is the medium through which a researcher collects a substantial dataset for analysis.

A thesis study is a study in which a researcher begins with a hypothesis that he either proves or disproves.

A *compare-and-contrast article* compares two topics, demonstrating similarities and differences between them.

An *opinion piece* is essentially a polemic, arguing for a particular point of view, which is supported by data.

Librarianship is a considered a social science, and its research literature heavily relies on statistical analysis. Because of this, it is wise for graduate students to learn Excel, SPSS, and similar programs, if these are offered at your school. However, becoming familiar with statistics and statistical packages is important for all librarians, not just those who seek careers in academia. One of the most common methodologies used in LIS is the survey. Generally, the author tests out his questions on colleagues and a sample group to make sure they are understandable and without bias. Once the questions are established, the author creates a survey and sends it to the participant pool. This can be easily done using a free app like Survey Monkey. When the survey is completed, the results are downloaded into Excel or another statistical package. Survey questions may be *quantitative* (Y/N) and or *qualitative* (requiring an individual response). The survey results generally are analyzed using descriptive and inferential statistics.

Another often used methodology is the focus group. A focus group consists of individuals who are chosen because they match particular criteria: for example, the focus group might consist of only sophomore students or only faculty from the English Department. As with the survey, the questions are pretested to make sure they are reliable and don't reflect bias. Focus groups are a form of *qualitative research.*

Managing the Journal Process

Managing the journal production process involves a number of steps. Many of these are behind the scenes, focused on the mechanics of moving articles from submission to review to layout, copy editing, proofreading, publication, and publicity. But the most important phase of this work is at the start, in the submission-to-review stage of this process. Setting up appropriate inputs to the review and publication process helps ensure that the outputs—what we publish—are appropriate to the journal and to our readers.

A journal's reputation lies almost exclusively in its ability to publish high-quality, well-written, original, and engaging information. Not every submitted article is ready for peer review when it comes in. How do I, as an editor, ensure that the inputs to the peer-review process are going to lead to quality outputs, after reviewers have done their critical work? Here are thing things I take into account.

- Readership—A journal has an established audience, but the established audience may not be the desired audience. There's a balancing act to make sure the content we publish is of interest to the core readership but also will attract readers who should be interested in the journal, but haven't found it yet.

- Technical quality of submission—An article needs to be clearly focused, well written, and presented in a professional style that allows any reader to follow the argument being made. One of the major advantages of publishing an online, open-source journal is that submissions come in from around the world, including from countries where English (the journal's language, and the primary language of the majority of the journal's readers) is not a native tongue. Some writing can be improved through light editing to improve clarity of communication; some writing is sufficiently opaque that a rewrite might be required before the article can be effectively peer-reviewed.

- Originality—In any narrowly defined field (such as library technology), there are a number of topics that come up repeatedly. Research needs to be original, or present a significantly different point of view or method, or (in some cases) confirm research already done through a replication study, in order to advance scholarship in the area. Being able to identify advances in a field, as opposed to repeated confirmation of well-understood challenges or issues, is important for the editor.

- Diversity of voices—It is important to the journal that the materials we publish represent the breadth of the profession. While we are an academic journal, and primarily attract research by individuals in academic settings (and often in pursuit of their own promotion or tenure processes), we are the journal of an organization of library professionals. Being able to represent the work of the library information technology profession is important, as the field is just divided enough to create artificial barriers between subspecialties (such as academic libraries, public libraries, and archives).

Kenneth J. Varnum,
Editor,
Information Technologies and Libraries

WHAT DOES A JOURNAL EDITOR LOOK FOR?

Editors of library journals are, for the most part, working librarians or academics. They edit professional and academic journals as a service to the profession. They are also human beings, who have their own likes and dislikes. If you do a comparison of the title pages of several library journals, you will see that each one is very different. Part of the reason for this is because the mission and audience of each journal is different, but it is also true that editors put their own stamp on a journal. An editor asks a number of questions before deciding to run an article that are purely mechanical. This makes sense for a number of reasons. If an editor of a journal that focuses on collection development receives an article on the "teaching library," he will most likely reject it out of hand, no matter how well it is written. If an editor for a top-tier, academic library journal receives an article that is only four pages long, he will send it back. Editors also want a variety or mix in the articles they run.

An editor will ask himself the following questions in deciding whether to accept or reject an article. These questions have nothing to do with the overall quality of the piece: What is the word count? Is the topic appropriate for the journal? Is the style of writing appropriate for the journal? Has a similar article run recently?

An editor also will ask the following questions that are specific to an author's work: Has the author satisfied the premise established in the lead paragraph of the article? If the author uses statistics, have these statistics been interpreted correctly? If the author has conducted a survey, are the results meaningful? If the author has done a literature review, is it adequate? Has the right citation style been used? Most importantly, an editor will ask himself whether an article needs revision. If there is too much work involved, the editor may simply return the manuscript to the author without comment. An editor, however, will work with a writer to improve a piece if it shows promise. If the author has submitted an article to a peer-reviewed journal, he will receive feedback from the individuals who have reviewed his work anonymously. If the reviewers accept a work with "minor revisions," an author often only needs to satisfy the reviewers' questions for his work to be published. Even if the reviewers indicate that the article needs "major revisions," the author may still have an opportunity to resubmit his manuscript.

You can improve your chances of getting published in various ways. Take a look again at the table of contents of journals that you would like to submit to. Can you engage in a dialogue with a controversial article that has recently run? Editors want to publish intelligent, well-written articles that provide different points of view about topical issues, such as linked data or the end of the brick-and-mortar library. Can you provide expertise on a topic? Editors value the work of knowledgeable writers. If you have organized an inventory project, created an advertising flyer for your library, or helped run an information literacy program, you are an authority on that topic.

Can you provide insight on an issue of general interest to libraries? If your library has recently gone through a reorganization, implemented major technical innovations, or is involved in a large fund-raising initiative, you may be able to comment on the significance of these activities for the larger community.

Before you submit your article to a publication, ask yourself the following questions. Have I picked the right article format? (If you are submitting a piece to a top-tier journal it probably will need to conform to one of the formats described earlier—a thesis study, a survey, a case analysis, or a literature review.) Have I picked the right tone? Have I picked the right publication? Have I followed the publication's guidelines for submission?

BOOKS AND BOOK CHAPTERS

If you are a LIS professor, you are usually required to have a doctorate in library science or in another related discipline. In this case, you probably are considering turning your dissertation into a book or your dissertation's chapters into a series of journal articles. The decision you make largely depends on the field you received your doctorate in. If it is in the humanities, a discipline in which the monograph is the most important channel for communication, you most likely will try to publish your thesis as a book. If your dissertation is in the social sciences, it is more likely that you will publish chapters as a series of peer-reviewed articles. In fact, graduate students in the social sciences often submit chapters of their dissertation for publication even before the manuscript is finished.

We are very lucky as a profession because there are so many venues for publication: there are specialized, refereed journals for school librarians, reference librarians, digital librarians, metadata specialists—almost every branch of librarianship. Commercial publishers as well as professional organizers, such as the American Library Association, publish on wide-ranging topics having to do with information studies as well. This strong publishing environment will make your chances for acceptance far greater than if you try to publish your dissertation in another discipline. Where you publish, however, is a decision you will have to make for yourself. If you are a Latin American Studies librarian, for example, your professional persona probably is tied closely to that discipline; it might make more sense for you to publish in that subject area.

Publishers resist releasing a dissertation "as is," and you will most likely be asked to do a significant revision. One reason is the nature of this type of scholarship. A dissertation is not structured as a book; rather, it is an exhaustive exploration of a disciplinary topic. In many fields the focus of a dissertation is so narrow that it in itself would not make a book that would appeal to either a specialized or general audience. If you do an online search for "academic publishers" or look through book catalogs, you should be able to find the publishing houses that are more closely aligned with your own interests. Every publisher also posts submission guidelines online. Most likely the publisher will require a cover letter, a brief CV, a description of your book, its audience, and its projected due date. If your proposal is accepted, you will be assigned an editor who will work with you in bringing your manuscript to fruition. Once it is finished, your book will be sent to one or two experts in your field to review.

Below is the author submission form used by ABC-CLIO/Librarians Unlimited, the publisher of the *Librarians' Guide to Professional Publication*.

AUTHOR SUBMISSION FORM

Before sending your proposal, please e-mail our acquisitions editors to review your ideas. Please provide the following information:

- Working title
- Purpose statement: explain the intent of the work, who it is for, and why it is needed
- Scope statement: describe the work's specific areas of coverage
- Objectives: identify the benefits readers will derive from the work
- Methodology: explain how you will research or compose the work
- Tentative outline: show how the work will be organized
- Competition or related works: identify similar titles and how your work will differ
- Approximate length (in pages or words)
- Résumé or bio statement: describe why you are qualified to write this book

SOLE-AUTHORED AND CO-EDITED BOOKS/CALL FOR BOOK CHAPTERS

Two other kinds of large publishing projects are sole-edited and co-edited books. An edited book is much easier to complete because it mainly involves the kind of project management skills we addressed in earlier chapters. However, a sole- or co-authored book generally has more prestige and is regarded more favorably if you are a professor or academic librarian. How do you know if you want to work with a co-editor or co-author? A book generally takes a year or more to produce, so you will want to consider how much time you have realistically to devote to this project, whether you have the specialized skills and contacts to do this your own, and whether you and your co-author or editor can work successfully together. Often the best people to collaborate with are those you have a professional but not close relationship with.

Book chapters are solicited in one of two ways. Either you are approached by a colleague who is editing a book and asks for your contribution, or you respond to a posting on a blog or list.

Below is an excerpt from a call for submissions for a technology book.

You are invited to submit a chapter proposal for the second edition of the successful and positively reviewed 2014 book published by ALA, *The Top Technologies Every Librarian Needs to Know*. Chapter proposals are due July 21, 2017, and can be submitted via the chapter proposal form.

Theme of the Book

What current technologies are on the cusp of moving from "gee whiz" to real-life application in libraries? This book will explore the information landscape as it might be in 3–5 years. It will describe the emerging technologies of today that are likely to be at the core of "standard" library offerings in the not-distant future. It will introduce project managers and project doers not just to new technologies, but it will also provide an understanding of the broader trends that are driving them.

Details

Chapters will be in the 4,000–4,500-word range and must address the following points:

1. Define the technology (in general, and in the context of the chapter).
2. Why does the technology matter in general, and to libraries in particular?
3. What are early adopters doing?

4. What does the future trend look like?

5. Having embraced this technology, what would the library of 2022 look like?

Proposals should be submitted to Ken Varnum, the book's editor, by July 21, 2017.

Timeline

July 21, 2017: Chapter proposals due via Call for Chapters Form
August 15, 2017: Authors notified of acceptance
December 15, 2017: Chapter drafts due
January 31, 2018: Editor's comments provided to authors
February 28, 2018: Revised drafts due to editor

SERVING AS AN EDITOR OF A BOOK

Because it takes both time and self-discipline to write a book, librarians often start as a book editor, either alone or with a co-editor. As a book editor, your job is to shepherd the book through the publishing process. You should be detail oriented, have good project management skills, and be able to establish a good rapport with your authors.

CHAPTER TAKEAWAY

This chapter describes the process of getting tenure at an academic institution. Although there are differences between the tenure requirements of LIS faculty and academic librarians on the tenure track, there are many similarities as well—the most important one being that the tenure applicant needs to have a game plan. The chapter also defines the most common types of research articles and provides strategies on how to get published.

NOTES

1. Marta Mestrovic Deyrup, "Web 2.0 and the Academic Library," *Technical Services Quarterly* 27 (2010): 145–150.

2. "Tenure Issues," AAUP, n.d., https://www.aaup.org/issues/tenure.

3. "Faculty Policies and Procedures Manual, 2017–2018," Longwood University, 2017, http://solomon.longwood.edu/media/academic-affairs/solomon/Final2017_18_FPPM.pdf.

4. "Tenure and Promotion," Syracuse University, Office of the Provost, n.d., http://provost.syr.edu/faculty-affairs/policies-and-procedures/tenure/.

APPENDIX

The Workbook

CHAPTER 1

1. Take a look at the University of Virginia Library's annual report (https://static.lib.virginia.edu/files/AR2014_web.pdf) and comment on the accessibility of the text to readers. Where do the graphics begin and where does the text? Which is more important in the telling of the narrative? For that matter, what is the narrative?

2. In the first chapter we established four "rules" of professional writing:

   Rule #1: Use the "good enough" principle.

   Rule #2: Before you start writing, ask yourself, what do I hope to gain?

   Rule #3: Don't reinvent what already exists.

   Rule #4: Think strategically.

   What kind of professional writing have you done so far? Do any of these tenets mirror your experience? Which do you think is the most important?

CHAPTER 2

1. Take the simple template below and see if you can modify it to reflect your own experiences.

Annual Report Template

Your name
Your department
Your job responsibilities
Your achievements this year
Personal goals met
Goals established for the next year

2. We've talked in this chapter about the tri-partite structure of most
    pieces of professional writing. The chart below reflects the "About Us"
    page of the Chicago Public Library Website. Find a similar library
    page on the Web and note what kind of writing "style" the author is
    using to get her point across.

Structure	Stylistic Devices
Introduction	Short sentences
Body of Text	Active verbs/present tense
Conclusion	Heightened language

CHAPTER 3

1. Find a blog that is related to your work. What makes the blog enjoy-
    able? The writing? The content? Could you duplicate a blog like this
    on your own?

2. Select one of the social media sites I've mentioned and analyze how it
    is being used as a communication tool. You might, for example, choose
    to analyze Georgia State University's library tour (https://www.you-
    tube.com/watch?v=Pd0noUli1MQ) in terms of the structure of its oral
    and visual narrative. How is it similar or different from a textual
    document?

3. Create a new document on your computer and pick a font we have
    not looked at. Type a sentence of your own using the font in bold,
    italic, and normal; choose different sizes of the fonts. Is there a
    difference in how you react to the different manifestations of the
    text?

CHAPTER 4

1. We've looked at several memos or memo-like documents in Chapter 4. Can you find similar examples from your own institution? If so, what do they have in common? Now see if you can create a template that would allow you to complete one of these memos by yourself.

2. How could you modify this example of an MOU and use it as a template for you own library's gift policy guidelines?

Policy for Large Gift Agreement

In order to create an environment of efficiency and usefulness, the Office of Collections has implemented the use of the memorandum of understanding for large and/or significant gifts. The purpose is to have the process in writing, a plan of action in place, and a timeline envisioned.

Library gifts-in-kind have the potential to greatly enrich our collections and the implementation of the memorandum of understanding seeks to expedite this process, thus in turn better serving our user community.

Librarian's information/librarian's name _____

Unit or library name: _____

E-mail: _____

Phone _____

Notes_____

Gift information: number of boxes of items_____

Number of items if applicable _____

Collection/donation description _____

Planning processing plan _____

Storage plan _____

3. The simple template for library meeting minutes consists of seven sections. Do your institution's meeting minutes follow this format or one similar to it? How far does yours stray from the template?

4. Create your own promotional materials for your library, using this template. Make sure your own writing style is one your patrons will respond to.

Dear (Community Business):

We need your help! The (Library Name) Library is offering a summer library program to the children of our community to encourage them to read for pleasure during the summer and to retain their reading skills. This year's theme is Dig into Reading.

To add to the fun and to create a sense of challenge that will keep kids reading, we'd like to offer incentives and contest prizes at various times during the summer. Because of our limited budget, we cannot afford to offer this without help.

We appreciate any donation you care to make. Possible donations include items to give away as prizes, small toys, coupons for free goods or services (admission tickets, fast-food coupons, free film, or film processing), or cash to buy prizes to offer as a Grand Prize. We will mention the assistance you have generously donated in our publicity.

If you can help us in any way, please contact me at the library (phone number). We hope to include you in our summer plans. Many thanks!

Sincerely,

CHAPTER 5

1. The basic template of a report is very simple. It consists of the following:

    *   Introduction
    *   Explanatory text (paragraphs 1, 2, 3 . . .)
    *   Conclusion/summary

    See if you can create a short but accurate summary of a personal report for yourself or a colleague

2. What kind of data-driven decisions does your library make? Are they based on quantitative or qualitative data, or both?

3. Keep track of your engagements on this weekly activity report. Study the times during the day when you don't have commitments and see whether any patterns are emerging? Can you find time to work on your professional writing projects during this free time?

Weekly Activity Report
(Please fill in daily and file on Friday afternoon)

Name:

Dates:

Objectives for the Week:

Activity

Saturday/Sunday:

Monday:

Tuesday:

Wednesday:

Thursday:

Friday:

Summary and Plans for Next Week:

CHAPTER 6

1. See if you can fill out this newsletter template for your own library.

    A Simple Newsletter Template

    - Welcome
    - Upcoming general programs and events
    - Upcoming teen programs and events
    - Upcoming children's programs and events
    - Library calendar
    - Report on new acquisitions and services

CHAPTER 7

1. Using this as a template, create or update your CV to fit your current job circumstances.

Contact Information

Name

Address

E-mail

Cell

Education

Reverse order: current to earliest; include year of graduation, university name, dates degrees were obtained (i.e., January 2012–present).

Employment

Reverse order: current to earliest; include name of company/organization; brief job description, dates of employment (i.e., January 2012–present).

Language(s) and Proficiencies

Include if appropriate.

Specialized Graduate Coursework, Training, or Certificates

Affiliations

Membership in civic, library, and other associations. Date range; position held.

CHAPTER 8

1. Can you tell what purpose these transitional words serve in the passage below? Are they setting up an opposition, a comparison, or a qualification of the text? What would happen if you substituted different words in their place?

    The more intertwined tasks and activities become, the more difficult it becomes to isolate any one task for the study. In the past, most theory and research presumed that the human activities involved in access to information could be isolated sufficiently to be studied independently. This is particularly true of information-seeking behavior, a process often viewed as beginning when a person recognizes the need for information and ending when the person acquires some information resources that address the need. Such a narrow view of the process of seeking information simplifies the conduct of research. For example, information seekers' activities can be studied from the time they log onto an information retrieval system until they log off with results in hand. The process can be continued further by following subsequent activities to determine which resources discovered online were used, how and for what purpose. Another approach is to constrain the scope of study to library-based information seeking. People can be interviewed when they first enter a library building to identify their needs as they understood them at that time. Researchers can follow users around the building (with permission of course) and can interview the users again before departure to determine what they learned or accomplished (excerpted from Christine Borgman, *From Gutenberg to the Global Information Infrastructure*, 7).

CHAPTER 9

1. Sometimes all you need to be a more effective writer is to modify your work habits. Think about those things that are preventing you from doing your best. Is it the time of day you've picked to write? Is your workspace too noisy or too quiet? Write down what changes, if any, would make you more productive.

CHAPTER 10

1. Do a skills inventory. Examine your job skills and responsibilities and ask yourself whether something you do, such as supervising or mentoring staff, teaching, or negotiating licenses, can form the basis of an article or presentation.

2. Using this example as a model, see if you can write your own scenario to come up with a beginning research agenda.

   Lois works part time at a local public library in Florida. She decides to create a reading list of YA books on race relations to spark discussion in the after-school program she started at the library. This booklist is featured on the library Web site. A reporter at a local newspaper sees it and asks Lois if he can write a news piece on her reading club. After it is published, the story is picked up by a local television show, and she is interviewed along with her reading group.

Result: Lois has now been asked to serve in a newly created position of youth services librarian and events coordinator in her town library.

Index

About the Author

MARTA MESTROVIC DEYRUP has worked as an editor, journalist, teacher, and for the last 20 years, as a librarian at Seton Hall University. Deyrup holds a PhD in Slavic languages and literatures from Columbia University and is the author or editor of several other books, including *Creating the High-Functioning Library Space: Expert Advice from Librarians, Architects, and Designers; Digital Scholarship*; and *Successful Strategies for Teaching Undergraduate Research*. For several years she taught the course "Writing for Publication" for the Simmons Graduate School of Library and Information Science in Boston, Massachusetts.